T0067992

A hat, a kayak
& dreams of Dar

A hat, a kayak
& dreams of Dar

TERRY BELL

First published in 2017 by Face2Face
An imprint of Cover2Cover Books
www.cover2cover.co.za
Copyright © Terry Bell

ISBN: 978-1-928346-64-7
e-ISBN: 978-1-928346-65-4

All rights reserved. No part of this publication may be reproduced,
stored in a retrieval system, or transmitted in any form or by any
means, electronic, mechanical, photocopying, recording or otherwise,
without the written permission of the publisher, except in accordance
with the provisions of the Copyright Act, Act 98 of 1978.

Design and cartography: Peter Bosman
Cover and book illustration: Ceiren Bell
Editing: Sandra Dodson
Proofreading: Clarity Editorial
Photo research and retouching: Brendan Bell

Printed by **novus print**, a Novus Holding company

PHOTO CREDITS
p 2 by permission, Allan Moult; p 26 copyright Press Association (PA)

Dedication

This book is dedicated to adventurers everywhere and especially to Kent Warmington, whose challenge and pursuit of the hat started us on this haphazard journey.

Contents

List of maps

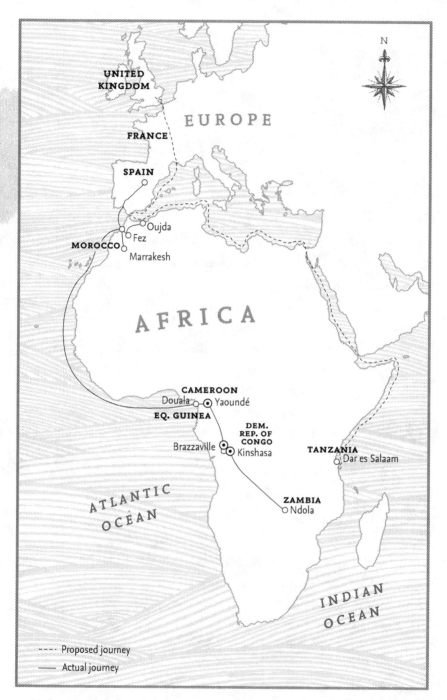

Dreams of Dar: proposed versus actual journey

Preface

Gentle reader,

You are about to embark on a most unusual adventure, in the company of two blithe-spirited, but highly principled, romantics. You will be taken back to the world of the 1960s, before mobile phones and laptops and low-cost flights. Back to a time when high-flown dreams could be launched, and the grisly realities they inevitably encountered often resulted in even more bizarre and colourful escapades. You will paddle across waters high and low; scrabble around the back streets of the Mediterranean world (both northern and southern shores); hitch-hike and travel in improbable vehicles across miles of desert; and live on bananas in Santa Isabel, Equatorial Guinea, before reaching the destination of East Africa.

I offer a word of introduction to the two characters you will be travelling with, whom Cervantes himself would have admired.

I met Barbara Edmunds and Terry Bell as fellow South African activists in Johannesburg in the early 1960s, when the drama of the Rivonia Trial was unfolding, Nelson Mandela was sentenced to life imprisonment and the security police were triumphant. In 1964 Terry and I found ourselves in adjacent cells in Pretoria Local Prison and cemented a friendship that has endured through many twists and turns over the past fifty years, as we episodically encountered each other in London, Zambia and the Cape. Terry and Barbara now live in Muizenberg, on Cape Town's South Peninsula, and I on the Atlantic Seaboard, in Hout Bay.

Terry is a prolific journalist, and the author of a serious and unsettling study of various raw and rancid matters left trailing in the wake of the defeat of apartheid: *Unfinished Business — South Africa, Apartheid and Truth*. A flamboyant personality, he is also a modest man. It was only after much urging that he and Barbara set pen to paper to tell us the inside story of their epic adventures as they attempted to canoe from Chiswick in London to Dar es Salaam in Tanzania in the fateful years of 1967/68. Barbara is more than the backroom partner here, even though her painstaking and detailed research forms the core of much of the writing. Hers is the steadying and guiding influence and, most importantly, the voice that is able to say "NO" when impossibilism threatens. We are all fortunate in that letters and recordings have survived that have made it possible for our canoeist authors to capture some of the immediacy and detail of their adventures, and bring to life the Dickensian array of characters they encountered.

It was normal for young South Africans of our generation to camp in the bush, cook food over an open fire, and think nothing of long-distance travel in ropey vehicles. But the Bell venture goes much further than this. There are undoubtedly vicarious pleasures ahead for those less inclined to spend their nights under open fishing boats on remote Spanish beaches. Or who wish to experience from the comfort of their armchairs the pleasures of third-class travel on *trenes de correo* or living in a shack in Gibraltar. There is also a serious historian of the battle sites of the oppressed struggling to emerge in Terry, which adds a further dimension of interest to this picaresque voyage.

Perhaps one day you, too, gentle reader, may seek to fulfil a dream.

Dr Sholto Cross *is a former political prisoner, exile, international consultant and was previously director of development studies at the University of East Anglia.*

Thanks

There are so many people — past, present and posthumous — to thank for the role they played in the production of this book. First and foremost is Barbara's late father, Rex Edmunds, who made up an album of every postcard we sent as we travelled. He also kept all the reel-to-reel taped messages we posted. Without these, fallible memory would not have been adequate to the task. Similarly, Kent Warmington's memory and habit of retaining letters over half a century were invaluable.

Over the years there have been numerous requests that we write this book. But it was John and Erica Platter who finally persuaded Barbara and me to get going. It was also their idea that we should include some of the recipes gathered and tried out en route. Still, nothing more would have happened had it not been for the enthusiastic reception of the idea by the great team at Cover2Cover Books.

Thanks must also go to Neville and Muriel Rubin for providing the modern *fluviacarte*, the map of the French waterways; to our photographer son, Brendan, who upgraded fifty-year-old photographs, and to our artist daughter, Ceiren, who provided line drawings to illustrate Barbara's section on canoe cuisine. Alide Dasnois provided invaluable advice as a reader of the first draft and we had an excellent editor, Sandra Dodson.

But it is to all those people in England, France, Spain, Gibraltar and Morocco who helped us — and often taught us more than they may have realised — that we owe a special debt of gratitude.

Terry & Barbara Bell

Prologue

In December 1964 I hitch-hiked from Johannesburg to Cape Town and back. Not once, but twice: a five-day journey covering 3,000 kilometres. I had the good fortune to be accompanied by Barbara Edmunds, whom I'd met a short while before. By the end of the trip I declared that she was the only person in the world I could travel with. She was great company and didn't mind walking long distances or standing on the roadside for hours on end. She was also a very good cook. And she never made a sarcastic remark about my olive green bush hat with its mock leopard-skin hatband.

I had been released from detention in August that year after nearly two months of solitary confinement under apartheid South Africa's ninety-day law. Aware that I was under fairly constant observation by the security police, I decided to adopt a peripatetic lifestyle. Hence the hitch-hiking adventure.

When another round of political arrests began, I made my way to Zambia. Barbara and I kept in touch and later met up in "Swinging Sixties" London, where I had been granted political asylum. Although there were lucrative scholarships and work available in London, I resented my deportation and was determined to get back to southern Africa, hoping to be on hand for what I thought would be imminent political change in South Africa. So when a friend challenged us to a long kayak journey, it seemed logical to return by canoe.

This book — or one like it — about a shambolic kayak voyage and the world's most travelled hat, was to have been completed forty-seven years ago. But the notes, manuscript drafts and rolls of film recording our adventure were stolen, along with virtually everything else we owned. We were left with no more than a passport, the clothes we

Posing before practice: the hat, the kayak (with painted boast) and the Bells

stood up in and a small amount of money. It was only eight years later, following the death of Barbara's father, that we fortuitously discovered he'd kept an album with all the postcards we'd sent to Barbara's parents during our travels. He had also kept the eleven reels of audiotape we'd posted. A few years ago we had the tapes transcribed onto CDs. Remarkably, after nearly half a century, all but one of those tapes were still audible.

Yet it was only in 2016, after a discussion about kayaking and writing with journalist and South African wine guide supremo John Platter, that we finally embarked on the writing of our story.

This book started as a tale about a kayak called *Amandla* and a haphazard voyage. But that olive green bush hat with its mock leopard-skin hatband assumed a character of its own and began to play a significant role in the story. Particularly after Kent Warmington, the

Canadian who had challenged me to canoe from London to Tangier, surfaced again via Facebook. He was historically acquainted with the hat, and he had kept our original correspondence.

Working on *A hat, a kayak and dreams of Dar* gave us considerable cause for reflection: on what was, what might have been and what is. We looked back nostalgically at those fundamentally hopeful days of the Sixties, when young people turned their backs on the old order and we seemed to be on the brink of a brave, new, democratic world. We marched in opposition to racism and militarism, supported nuclear disarmament and envisioned an era of peace, love and plenty, notwithstanding the slogan "turn on, tune in, drop out". We were sure apartheid South Africa would soon fall and America would suffer an ignominious defeat in Vietnam.

Revisiting this time in our lives, we were reminded not only how naive and recklessly adventurous youth can be, but how much enjoyment can be had, even in very difficult circumstances. Above all, how much can be learned.

I hope that you gain as much from reading our tale as Barbara and I did researching and writing it. For the record, we recently discovered that the part of Madrid where we searched for days for, among other things, my stolen headgear now has a backpacker hostel named "The Hat".

Terry Bell
Cape Town, 2017

CHAPTER 1

A hat on the hippie trail

I blame the Eskimos. Specifically the two Inuit fishermen who in 1965 were swept by stormy seas from Greenland to the north of Scotland in their sealskin kayaks. Their fortuitous landings made a small item of national news in Britain, and one of the newspapers carrying the report reached us in Tangier in Morocco. Then the hat got involved.

It was December 1965, in a smoke-filled room on the second floor of the Hotel Chaouen in the medina — the "Arab quarter" of Tangier. My girlfriend, Barbara Edmunds, and I, both recently exiled South Africans, were seeking respite in a warmer climate before returning to London. Also in the smoke-filled room were a couple of American Vietnam war draft dodgers and several Canadians.

An earnest and largely uninformed debate erupted. This concerned not the Inuit, but the merits of kayaks as opposed to what the Canadians present referred to as "Indian canoes".

Fuelled no doubt by the bottles of cheap Moroccan wine that passed from hand to hand and by the acrid fog emanating from those who puffed at pipes containing (technically illegal, but freely available) hashish, it ended with a challenge: that I could not paddle a kayak from London to Tangier.

The person who issued the challenge was Kent Warmington, a Canadian from Vancouver.

I had read somewhere that kayaks, with their centres of gravity below the water level, were the most stable of craft. With utter confidence I stated that, even without the experience of the Inuit, I could paddle from London to Tangier in a kayak, using rivers and canals and by following the coast.

It was one of those bold claims that might have been forgotten in the days, weeks and months to come. But then the hat got involved.

I had left South Africa and hitch-hiked my way to Zambia wearing my olive green bush hat with its mock leopard-skin hatband. I was deeply attached to that hat; it was as much a part of me when I travelled as a ticket or even a passport. It was the travelling headgear I had worn when hitching around South Africa. Even at night, stuffed with socks and underwear, it had served as a pillow. And it had accompanied me, via Nairobi, Khartoum, Rome and London, to Morocco.

On that fateful night in Tangier it hung on a bedpost, where it was admired by some of the group sitting on the beds or on the floor. A few, mainly men, were part of the motley crew travelling the hippie trail from Marrakesh and Tangier in the West, through Spain and France and on to Kabul in Afghanistan. Some, like Kent, were committed travellers. Others were mainly "plastic hippies", playing the part during a summer vacation, or Americans dodging military service.

One of the Canadians, "Murphy", was especially smitten by the hat. He offered to buy it — in dollars. I refused. But as we cleared the empty wine bottles from the room the next morning, we noticed that the hat was missing.

In that small travelling community it was not difficult to find out what had happened: the Canadian who had admired the hat had taken it and boarded the morning ferry for Spain. He was wearing it and seemed to be heading off on the hippie trail to Kabul.

I raged about "thieving Canucks". This seriously upset Kent.

"I'll get your hat back for you," he promised.

We had to return to London for the start of the following week, to studies and to work. But Kent was confident. Everybody knew the hippie trail and there were only so many places along the route where travellers would stop, he said. So Barbara gave him the London address where she was staying with an aunt and we prepared to hitch-hike back.

Months went by and we heard nothing from Kent. By that time Barbara was teaching and helping me as I edited the monthly *Anti-Apartheid News* and campaigned in support of the first strike by British seamen since 1911. After decades of long hours of work and low pay, British seafarers, members of the National Union of Seamen (NUS), had stopped work, demanding better wages and a reduction in the working week from fifty-six to forty hours. The Labour government under Harold Wilson reacted by declaring a state of emergency and the NUS called for solidarity. So every Saturday throughout the strike — the one day we had free — Barbara would hand out leaflets in support of the seafarers while I addressed crowds in street markets, standing on a soapbox and detailing the plight of the maritime workers.

It was a hectic period, since I was also a full-time university student. All thoughts of the kayak challenge had evaporated.

Then one Saturday morning, among the millions of people in London, I thought I spotted Kent just ahead of me, going up the crowded stairs at Earl's Court underground station. I couldn't be sure, so I decided to call out his name. If it wasn't him, nothing would happen; English people, I had discovered, paid no heed to displays of eccentricity.

But it *was* Kent. He stopped and turned around, to the obvious annoyance of others tramping up the stairs. Then, without any greeting, he yelled, "So, did you get your hat?"

I rushed up to him and together we elbowed our way out into the street.

"My hat? What do you mean?"

"I found it. Bought it back. Got it parcelled up and posted it," Kent said. But he was in a hurry, late for work. "It's a long story," he added as we exchanged addresses. "I'll come round and tell you tonight."

Barbara and I were by then sharing an apartment in the west London suburb of Chiswick with one of Barbara's fellow teachers. And that night, as promised, Kent arrived with a story that almost made me feel I owed it to him to paddle to Tangier.

Kent had followed the hat and its thieving wearer from Spain, through Europe, all the way to Afghanistan, asking at every youth hostel and crash pad about a Canadian called Murphy and that hat. Travellers' tales of the hat-wearing Murphy accumulated. Doubtless, Murphy also heard about a crazy Canadian pursuing him for the hat.

Kent finally traced the hat to a guesthouse in the Afghan town of Ghazni, some 150 kilometres south of Kabul. There was a dormitory room where, he was told, several foreigners were living. One of them was a young American who said that Murphy had left two days earlier. But when Kent told him the story of the hat, the American confessed that, as Murphy left, he had sold the hat to him. He would sell it back to Kent for the $6 he had paid for it.

"I paid the American with my last American one-dollar bills and set off as quickly as I could for Kabul and a post office," Kent said.

Using a UN food aid rice bag, he had packaged the hat and posted it — to the wrong address in London. He had mixed up the number of the apartment with the street number.

It was a sad denouement. I thanked him for the extraordinary efforts he had gone to and vowed not to give up my search.

Shortly after our chance encounter, Kent left for Canada. Within weeks we received a package from Vancouver, from the very same Kent Warmington. Inside the box was the UN rice bag containing the hat. When he'd posted the bag from Kabul, he'd given as his return address the Canadian High Commission in London. And when the wrongly addressed parcel was sent on to the High Commission, officials eventually looked up Kent's particulars and discovered that he had returned to Canada. So the High Commission posted the bag to Vancouver and Kent boxed it and forwarded it again.

I was ecstatic. I wrote immediately and effusively to Kent, a letter he kept and forwarded to me nearly fifty years later when we had again made contact. I declared the hat to be "a vital key to my existence ... [It] sweats Istanbul, Tehran, Kabul, Vancouver, right through my scalp... My brain is becoming permeated with the desire to follow the lead of my hat. And this I shall do."

Barbara, too, thought this some sort of omen, although we both quickly assured ourselves that we were not superstitious.

"Let's celebrate by taking the weekend off and going camping," I said.

Not being at all familiar with the English coast, I chose the first seaside town that came to mind — Hastings. Barbara agreed. The next weekend we packed up our tent and camping gear and hit the road, my hat on my head. A black Morris Oxford gave us a lift from the outskirts of London.

In the car I doffed my hat and got chatting with the driver, a draughtsman working for British Gas. It was a pleasant drive and the weather was good. He dropped us off at the turnoff to Hastings, and only when he had driven away did I realise — I had left my hat in the car. The reason for our celebratory weekend had sped off up the road. Where to we did not know.

Somewhat depressed, we set up camp on the cliffs above Hastings, spent the weekend there and hitched back to London on the Sunday. First thing on Monday I started telephoning every British Gas depot listed looking for a draughtsman who drove a black Morris Oxford car. I found him, and the hat came back again.

And so our busy lives in London resumed against the backdrop of Carnaby Street, the Beatles and the liberating influence of the Pill. By now we were deeply involved in work, studies and political activity. In addition to the great Seamen's Strike of 1966, it was the time of Vietnam War protests and Campaign for Nuclear Disarmament marches.

It wasn't long before we both felt we needed a break. If the olive green bush hat could have such adventures, why shouldn't we? I was still annoyed at having been forced out of Africa. Landing in

"Swinging Sixties" London via a series of unexpected circumstances did not seem to compensate.

"Why not take up Kent's kayaking challenge?" I suggested to Barbara. "In fact, why not extend it and go on to Dar es Salaam?"

Dar es Salaam in Tanzania was a base of exiled resistance to apartheid and the translation of the name (Haven, or abode, of Peace) was redolent of the hopes we shared. Besides, I wanted to get back to Africa, specifically to the southern African countries — later called the Frontline States — that supported the anti-apartheid struggle. This would mean that when (never if) the real fightback began in South Africa, we could be on hand to take part.

We could paddle down the Thames, cross to France, take the canals and rivers to the Mediterranean and then follow the coasts of Europe and North Africa. Then up the Nile, portage to Port Said and so on into the Red Sea, around the Horn of Africa and down to Dar es Salaam.

Barbara was not impressed, so, to strengthen my case, I wrote to the Royal Marines about the prospects for such a trip. Yes, they replied, it was perfectly feasible. However, in the area around the Red Sea and the Horn, there was a danger of piracy; it was probably best not to be armed and not to carry much of value. From their response it was obvious that they thought we were accomplished canoeists.

This was something I was sure we would become.

That sealed it for me, but Barbara had another suggestion: "Let's go by bicycle and start in Scandinavia."

I was unmoved. And I held the trump card. In the debate with Kent she had agreed that a kayak trip to Tangier was feasible. So the die was cast, although she did not then mention an abiding wariness of the sea and an acute susceptibility to seasickness.

CHAPTER 2

How to escape without a passport

For as long as I can remember I have enjoyed travelling — by foot, car, train or any other means. But at nineteen it became clear to me that, because of political activism, I would not be given a passport by the South African authorities. So, while I had visited a fair amount of South Africa by the time I was twenty, I knew I had little prospect of becoming a legitimate international traveller.

At the time I was working as a journalist at the Johannesburg *Star* newspaper. In South Africa in the 1960s, newspaper managements and editors on the larger newspapers applied to the police for press cards for their reporters. These carried a photograph of the journalist. I had thought until then that my very minor anti-apartheid political activities had gone unnoticed. They obviously hadn't. The management of the Johannesburg *Star* applied for my card as a court reporter and it was refused. So there was no prospect of getting a passport.

However, I discovered that there existed something called a "Protectorates Travel Document". It looked like a passport and allowed farmers on the borders of the country to travel into neighbouring states for up to ten days, apparently to search for strayed livestock. It could also be issued on an urgent basis, which I hoped would mean that it did not require police clearance. So I applied for one, claiming extreme urgency, and picked it up hours later without the usual security police interview.

To check that it would work, at least with neighbouring states, I booked some leave, shouldered my rucksack, put on my newly acquired bush hat and hitch-hiked to Swaziland. I had no trouble with my "passport" either entering or leaving the country, even though I had no cattle in tow on my return.

When, in July and August 1964, I was detained and interrogated by the security police, I managed to hide the document as they searched my apartment, retrieving it when I emerged from Pretoria Local Prison. Then, when another crackdown on anti-apartheid activists appeared to be looming, I decided to leave South Africa and make my way to newly independent Zambia.

Armed with my Protectorates Travel Document, I set off in April 1965, my departure coinciding with the annual Easter "rush" across the Beitbridge border post into what was then Southern Rhodesia. Just north of Pretoria I was given a lift by a Dutch Reformed Church minister, a *dominee*, Rev Du Toit. I couldn't believe my luck: no official would think of questioning someone travelling with a Dutch Reformed Church minister. Moreover, we were probably distantly related. When I gave my mother's name as Du Toit Joubert, we went through a lengthy discussion about the families, going back to 1688.

Rev Du Toit was driving up to a church mission in Fort Victoria (Masvingo). I was heading for Salisbury (Harare).

"How fortunate," he said, and explained that he was only stopping over at the mission for the night and would go on to Salisbury the next morning. I could stay over at the mission and he would drop me off in Salisbury after breakfast.

This was luck in spades. I was behaving impeccably, having doffed my hat respectfully when he first picked me up. Just as well, since he insisted on intoning a prayer for safe travel before we drove off.

Inside the border post I took my hat off again and placed it on the long counter where I, and perhaps twenty or thirty people, including Rev Du Toit, had to fill in the official forms. Here I was on my own; nobody would realise that I was with Rev Du Toit. I nervously completed the form, stating that I was on a visit for a week, and presented it at the counter along with my document. It was looked at, then stamped, and I was waved on my way.

With my stomach still churning, I walked across to the car where

11

Rev Du Toit was already waiting. That bridge across the Limpopo River signalled freedom.

But when we got to the other side I realised that I had left my hat behind.

"Oh, my boy, but you *must* go back and fetch it," said the *dominee*.

I protested. It was completely unnecessary. I could always buy another hat. I didn't want to delay the good reverend. But he insisted. What could I do? And so I embarked on what I remember as the longest walk of my life, back into South Africa to fetch my hat. I felt physically ill as I re-entered the border post.

The hat was there where I had left it. I pointed at it, to nobody in particular, as the reason for my return, slammed it onto my head and, once out of the door, ran full tilt back across the bridge to where the *dominee* was waiting. He was as good as his word. I slept over at the mission and was dropped off in Salisbury.

With only R13 to my name, I needed a job, and I soon discovered that there were jobs going in Zambia. But my document didn't cover Zambia. However, with all the blind optimism of youth, I telephoned the editor of Zambia's national daily newspaper in Ndola and applied for a job as a sub-editor. The editor of what was then the *Northern News* — soon to become the *Times of Zambia* — offered to telegraph the required £150 deposit to the Chirundu border post to allow me entry.

I brazened it out at Chirundu and my lookalike passport passed muster. Illegally in Zambia, I hit the road to the Copperbelt town of Ndola. There were some startled looks when I walked into the newsroom. Perhaps because I wore blue jeans tucked into brown calf-length paratrooper boots; a belt adorned with an axe and a sheathed "Black Forest" dagger; a rucksack; a bead-handled stock whip dangling from my left wrist; and the hat as the *pièce de résistance*. It was my idea of the fully equipped, ready-for-anything traveller which Rev Du Toit had obviously accepted as perfectly normal.

The newspaper needed anyone who knew his or her way around a newsroom, but also someone whose English accent could be understood by Zambians. The company had recruited an experienced journalist from England as a senior reporter, but he was a Geordie, from Newcastle upon Tyne. His English, the Zambians complained, sounded like a foreign language. So I took his job and he filled the vacancy as a sub-editor.

As the chief reporter of the country's national daily, I made a wide range of contacts that later stood me in good stead. I also corresponded with Barbara, whom I had met in Johannesburg the previous December. I missed her; she was more than just a friend and convivial travelling companion and I hoped we would meet up again. She had also become concerned about the way things were developing in South Africa. As a result, she was planning to spend a year or two working in England. Initially refused a passport, she characteristically protested and was finally issued with one, valid for a single year. She decided to leave for London in November 1965.

In the meantime, my post as chief reporter on what had become the *Times of Zambia* was made permanent. So I put in an application to become an official Zambian resident. This required that I submit my "passport". I confidently did so, in the naive belief that there would be no close scrutiny of the document. I was wrong. I was officially informed about something I already knew: that I had entered the country illegally. My application for residence was turned down.

I appealed against the decision. Meanwhile, the South African police requested that I be extradited to South Africa. President Kenneth Kaunda reacted by rejecting the request and stating that he was seeking political asylum for me in other countries for my "own personal safety".

It sounded very grand and elevated me to a prominence I did not deserve. The fact was that Zambia was dealing with a massive influx of refugees from Mozambique and Angola at the time. If the Zambian government allowed me to stay, it would set a precedent. Thousands of Angolans and Mozambicans fleeing warfare in their countries could also claim residence in Zambia. I had to be told that I would be given refuge elsewhere.

And that was how, armed only with a letter from the British High Commissioner in Lusaka, I landed in London in August 1965. I still had my hat, my rucksack and my boots, along with a slightly larger wardrobe, including a suit, dress shirts and a tie.

When I disembarked at Heathrow Airport, I was simply waved through. It was early morning and there were very few people about in the airport terminal, so I made my way to a bus going to Victoria station, missing a welcome party of people who had campaigned to have the British government grant me asylum.

After a couple of weeks wandering around the city, staying at the YMCA and in various "squats" in north London, I landed a job on the *Daily Mail* as part of an investigative team.

I had a haircut, donned my suit and tie, and, bearing the "Alien's Book" issued by the British Home Affairs department, I started work and made contact with other exiles. From them I discovered that there were substantial bursaries available for South African exiles who wished to study.

And so I became a "United Nations Fellow" enrolled in a diploma course in international affairs at London's University College. All fees were paid, we received US$100 a year for books and the £50 a month tax-free stipend was the equivalent at the time of the average railway worker's gross wage. At the same time I began editing the monthly *Anti-Apartheid News* and worked at night as a freelance sub-editor.

When Barbara arrived to take up a teaching job in north London, we got together again. She was staying with an aunt in Paddington, and I would visit her there frequently. Socialising together, we became part of the small but vibrant South African exile scene as she waited for her teaching placement in the new year. In the process, we discovered that we had even more in common than we had thought.

As December 1965 dawned, the reality of a British winter set in. I made my way to a telephone and rang Barbara. Since it was the university Christmas break and her job was due to start only in January, would she like to head somewhere warm? Yes, she would. How about Morocco? I asked.

Barbara's passport was still valid until September of the following year. I had a "stateless person's document": four large, yellow pages with my photograph and a declaration that I was under the protection of Britain. My nationality was "South African N/D", which I assumed meant "Not Determined". It was these documents that we used when we travelled to Tangier, met Kent and accepted the kayaking challenge.

But in September 1966, Barbara also became effectively stateless. When she went to the South African Embassy to renew her passport, it was refused. She, like me, found herself in exile.

As luck would have it, I discovered shortly after this that I could become an Irish citizen. A fellow exile, Geoff Lamb, informed me that he had become Irish though marriage to someone of Irish descent.

"Haven't you got some Irish in you?" Geoff asked.

Indeed I had Irish ancestry: a grandfather, my father's father, who had died decades before I was born. So I duly wrote to the General Register Office (*Oifig An Ard-Chláraitheora*) in Dublin. Then, with the requisite birth and marriage certificates proving my paternal ancestry, I went to the Irish Embassy and became a citizen of the Republic of Ireland.

After that it was plain sailing. On Friday, 30 September 1966, Barbara and I took a day off work and lectures and got married in the Hounslow Register Office. That made her Irish, too.

Saint Patrick was on our side.

CHAPTER 3

A kayak called *Amandla*

As the first colony in which the native people fought for and won independence from Britain, Ireland had a generally unsullied international relations reputation. And the Irish had certainly travelled. The country's greatest export had been the labour, skills and talents of millions of its citizens. An Irish passport was acceptable everywhere that officialdom was aware that Ireland existed. In travel terms, Irish citizenship and an Irish passport meant that the world was now open to us.

But it was Africa that beckoned.

With our Irish passports now only an application away and my hat back in its rightful place, a kayak journey from London to Dar es Salaam seemed entirely plausible. Even if it took us two years to cover the 7,000 miles (11,000 kilometres) to Tanzania, the adventure seemed worth it — to me at any rate.

Barbara and I assiduously put aside money from our respective salaries, and in August 1966, with the help of my study grant, I ordered a 16-foot (4.9-metre) twin-cockpit, glass-fibre kayak from a Richmond boat builder. But my grandiose ideas of having outriggers fitted, along with a sail, were quickly put down by the boat builder. He was obviously a kayaking purist, and he grumpily dismissed my suggestions.

Perhaps he knew nothing of the outriggers used on the great canoes of Polynesia, which I had read about. But I lacked the confidence to argue. Especially since he conceded the sail. And he pointed out that all that was necessary was leeboards. These operated like the fins on twin-keeled yachts. They were fitted on either side of the kayak, on a wooden bar fixed between the two cockpits, and could be swivelled down into the water and fixed in position. Under sail, they would apparently stop the craft from capsizing.

The following month we took delivery of the white-hulled and blue-decked kayak we named *Amandla*, meaning "Strength" or "Power" in Zulu and Xhosa. We aimed to leave on our great voyage in early July of the following year, as soon as my final exams were over.

"But we are going to have to practise," said Barbara.

With nearly ten months before our planned departure, I assured her we would have plenty of time to get used to the kayak on the river. In any event, I was sure we would be able to "learn as we go". We would be able to take our time down the River Thames and around the coast before tackling the canals and waterways of France, which I was certain would be a joy. I had read quite a bit about the canals, largely in relation to my interest in World War I. So I assured Barbara that it would be idyllic — paddling through history.

In the process we would be able to iron out any problems and discard, add or replace items. Having been a summer of relatively clement weather, even the challenge of the Channel seemed to pose no problem: we could bide our time and cross with one of the mass canoe crossings I had heard about.

"Why, even school kids do it," I assured my still-sceptical partner.

By the time we reached the Mediterranean, I was sure we would have become more than just adept at handling the kayak. It would be a summer cruise to and along "the Med" by two (by then) highly accomplished paddlers.

So it was that I never found the time to rig out the interior of the vessel or to adequately waterproof the rear stowage, let alone strengthen the bottom of the hull that would be run aground as we landed on beaches every night. These were all things I knew should be done. But I could not see that it mattered. We would be able to stop off for weeks if necessary to have "everything fixed up" before tackling the major part of the trip, which, in my blinkered optimism, always seemed to start in Tangier.

We managed to paddle out into the Thames on a couple of occasions before the winter of 1966 set in. We would manoeuvre *Amandla* onto the fold-away cradle provided by the boat builder, then wheel her from our High Street flat above a plant shop, through the Cromwell Road extension underpass and down to the slipway, mostly at high tide.

On several of those occasions we paddled downriver to Hammersmith and called in at the famous Dove pub, according to local lore a notorious smugglers' inn in the early eighteenth century. It was said that smugglers' ships would come up the river on a full tide at night and tie up alongside the Dove. As the tide turned, the dropping water level would expose a hidden cellar entrance through which the untaxed casks of wine and other booty would be passed. By the time the revenue men turned up to check, the ship would contain no taxable cargo and, the tide having risen again, there would be no sign of the underwater entrance.

We loved the story. And we loved the pub. We had never developed a taste for the warm, flat beverage the English call beer, and the Dove in those days had another attraction — Old Harry. Also made by the local Fuller's Brewery, it was a bottled brown ale that we would sit and sip while watching the river traffic passing by, *Amandla* bobbing alongside. It was a great way to spend a late September Sunday afternoon, but it didn't do much for our canoeing prowess.

On only one occasion before the spring of 1967 did we venture further east than the Hammersmith Bridge, just a few kilometres downriver from the slipway in Chiswick. That was on what we termed our "honeymoon cruise", after our marriage in the Hounslow Register Office: an extremely low-key affair, with just the two of us and my parents as witnesses. My father had recently retired after thirty-seven years working on the railways, and he and my mother had decided to visit Europe. They were staying with us.

Barbara's parents, whom I had never met, were both devout Anglicans and had put considerable pressure on her — in letters and even a few telephone calls —to marry in a church. My parents expressed no opinion, but were happy to be our witnesses. And so the deed was done and we decided that the rest of the day would be taken up by a "honeymoon in the East".

We got the high street photographer to take a picture for Barbara's parents and arranged to pick it up the following week. Then we rushed back to the flat, changed and trundled *Amandla* down to the slipway. We didn't quite get the tides right, but spent a very enjoyable few hours on the water paddling toward London's East End and then back to Chiswick.

All too soon the chills of winter arrived and *Amandla* had to be stored. We hung her up on large wooden pegs I had attached to the wall beside the alleyway entrance to our flat. And our rather hectic lives went on.

In the meantime, the brother of one of our fellow exile friends heard the story of my hat and turned up on the doorstep bearing a gift — a hat for Barbara. It was roughly the same design, but a light khaki colour and with a genuine springbok-skin band, the left side clipped up, military style. Further proof, I announced, that we were destined to paddle off together.

As the summer of 1967 approached, we did take *Amandla* out again from time to time, but I'd still done nothing about building waterproof storage compartments. Such details, I remained convinced, could be dealt with once we were on our way. When we had said farewell to friends and set off, we could take our time making the finishing touches. Then, as we were about to cross the strait to Tangier, perhaps we would be able to sell some features to magazines or newspapers about our travels and travails. The odd canoeing, camping or yachting publication might also be interested in us. At any rate there would probably be little interest in us until we had, perhaps, reached Gibraltar.

To cover this eventuality, in May I arranged with a small news feature agency to handle any material I might write and photograph en route. I also decided to put out a brief press release about the trip in the hope that if one or two newspapers picked up on it, they might later buy the odd feature article offered by the agency. I planned to follow it up with another press release shortly before we paddled off in July. From the point of view of our haphazard scheme, my timing could not have been more disastrous.

The two-paragraph notice of our intention to paddle from London to Dar es Salaam went out to the Press Association and various newspapers for the last weekend in May. And it was on that Sunday, 28 May, that Francis Chichester, the first man known to have sailed single-handed around the world, arrived in the port of Plymouth. Media mayhem erupted, some of the attention spilling over onto the prospect of us paddling from London to Dar es Salaam. And it was Barbara who had to deal with it.

I was in the final stretch of my university course and was still working nights as a sub-editor. Home from school in the afternoons, Barbara found herself confronted by yachting correspondents from the national media asking her questions about the extent of our canoeing experience and wondering whether we might use a drogue.

Barbara didn't have a clue what was meant by a drogue. Neither did I, but a library visit revealed that a drogue is a sea anchor attached to the stern and designed to slow a boat in a storm and keep the hull perpendicular to the waves. We would not be using one.

Fortunately, in those less gender-sensitive days, Barbara was able to fob off such queries with a perfunctory "My husband deals with that". And of course I was not around.

"All this will soon die down," I assured Barbara, in a classically flawed perception of the immediate future. It was today's news and, I smugly remarked, "Today's news is tomorrow's fish and chips paper."

But then calamity struck: Barbara's father, in Johannesburg, had a heart attack. He was in a critical condition. In those days before mobile phones, we had to wait.

"Perhaps we should put off the trip until next year," Barbara suggested. "You could carry on at university," she added, since I had been offered both a place and an extension of the quite lucrative grant.

But that meant another two-year commitment and I had had enough of the mid-1960s London environment. Despite its swinging image, London was fundamentally staid. Beneath a thin veneer of gloss, glitter and seemingly alternative lifestyles, there was a solid core of smug conservatism. But the real reason for my obduracy was that I had committed us to the trip by telling our friends that we would leave by kayak in 1967. I felt I could not back down.

As July dawned it became obvious that Chichester mania had only just begun. When it comes to pomp and pageantry, especially involving royalty and the grand imperial past, nobody can beat the English. What happened in that month underlined for me the importance of understanding history and the legacy — the baggage — it carries into the present and the future.

We accepted that Chichester would be knighted. That was what the English did. But what never dawned on me at the time was that this would be by the second Queen Elizabeth. The first Elizabeth to sit on the throne had also knighted a sailor who had circumnavigated the globe —Francis Drake. Two Elizabeths, 386 years apart, and two sailors named Francis, who epitomised the claimed "hearts of oak" that had conquered "again and again". It was a nationalist and royal public relations bonanza. So it was that on 14 July 1967, *Gipsy Moth IV*, the 16-metre (53-foot) ketch that had borne Chichester around the world, replicated the arrival in 1581 of Francis Drake's *Golden Hind* at the quay in Greenwich.

With thousands of flag-waving spectators present, Francis Chichester stepped ashore and walked up a red carpet to be greeted by Queen Elizabeth II and Prince Philip. Francis Chichester then knelt before his monarch and she touched him on the shoulders with the same sword that had dubbed Francis Drake as she bade Sir Francis Chichester, Knight Commander of the British Empire, to rise.

I almost felt relieved that Barbara's father's illness had delayed our departure. To leave in *Amandla* in the midst of this publicity, some of which would certainly include us, was out of the question. Quite apart from the fact that we were far from ready, we were also probably incapable of putting on an even halfway reasonable show of competence.

"As long as we get going before the end of August, we can still make it to the Mediterranean before winter really sets in," I confidently told Barbara.

Meanwhile, Barbara shopped for what she considered essential for her "kitchen". "You can look after the rest," she said.

In 1963, Nikon had brought out the Nikonos, a 35 mm camera that could be used underwater and was, therefore, weatherproof and incredibly tough. I checked the literature, sought one out, and bought a Nikonos. It would be an essential way of documenting our journey. I also bought a lightweight tent, lifejackets, two bright orange weatherproof anoraks and a small hand-held compass. I had still not decided what to do about storage compartments, but knew I had to protect my typewriter, paper and film. So I also bought a couple of large, heavy-duty plastic chart cases. Finally, at Barbara's insistence, we each bought a pair of lightweight and rope-soled canvas "yachting shoes" and heavy, "greasy wool", roll-neck jerseys.

"You should make a list," said Barbara. "Otherwise how do you really know what we'll need?"

I thought it an unnecessary question. We would find out exactly what we needed as we travelled and would adjust accordingly.

I was about to learn some very hard lessons.

CHAPTER 4

A shambolic departure from Chiswick

University was over and in the middle of August Barbara's father received a medical all-clear. I think it was only then that reality dawned on me. I had committed to leaving within weeks; there was no way out of it now and I hadn't even got around to handing in our applications for passports.

Barbara, on the other hand, had all her equipment ready: paraffin stove, mugs, plates, billy-can pots with their frying-pan lids and numerous bottles of herbs and spices, some stowed neatly in empty film containers. Also plenty of towels.

"Where do we put everything?" was all she wanted to know.

So began a lengthy period of packing, unpacking and re-packing. It must have been the best part of a week before we had some idea of how everything would be stowed. With hindsight, it was something of a shambles, but I kept assuring myself — and repeating to Barbara — that everything would work out perfectly once the journey was underway.

The fact that we were about to leave — and the manner of our leaving — also meant that our comrades from the exile community and friends from university seemed constantly to come around, often resulting in impromptu "leaving parties".

We decided to catch the mid-morning high tide at Chiswick on Monday, 21 August. Before this I would have to take the passport applications and photographs to the Irish Embassy. A Mr O'Rourke was not impressed by my tardiness when I told him that we needed our passports in a hurry because we were about to paddle to Dar es Salaam. But he issued a dual passport (a single document covering both of us) along with the advice, "You realise we don't have much diplomatic representation around the world, so don't be getting into any trouble."

By then the interest in Chichester seemed to have subsided, having climaxed with the issue of a set of stamps on 24 July. But I still wanted to make some money writing en route, so I put out the long-promised, final, brief press release — another mistake. Even before we had finished packing and left the backyard to start the long trundle down to the river, we were inundated. We had expected a group of fellow ANC Youth League members and university friends to see us off, but what happened was a media circus.

There were TV cameras, journalists and curious members of the public jostling with singing, chanting comrades, among them a future president and several individuals destined to become cabinet ministers in post-1994 South Africa. To cap it all, we were still trying to pack some of the odds and ends that had somehow been forgotten.

But we eventually made it into and across the high street, through the underpass and down to the river. There more interviews began and a little old woman we had never seen before burst into tears as she hugged each of us in turn and wished us Godspeed. We also had to rescue our paddles from our jubilant comrades and by then the tide had well and truly turned.

Somehow we managed to get into the kayak, only to be held back by demands for more photographs.

Some items were getting in the way.

"Just throw them out," I whispered to Barbara, seated in the front cockpit.

And so we threw out the sail and, to our later — and greater — regret, the paper-powered portable barbeque.

As we paddled away from the Chiswick shore, into six days that still remain largely a blur, Barbara pointed out that we were now hours too late to take full advantage of the tide.

"Never mind," I assured her. "Once we leave this lot behind, we'll find a quiet place to pull up and sort everything out."

I was wrong. On every bridge we paddled under, there was at least one photographer. And the wind was against us, although we still

S.A. couple on two-year canoe voyage

From Our Correspondent
London, Tuesday.

LOOKING RIDICULOUSLY FRAIL, wobbling dangerously and lying low in the water, a 16½ft. canoe, spurred on by loud chanting from members of South Africa's banned African National Congress, has started on its journey down the Thames on the first leg of a proposed 7,000-mile trip to Dar es Salaam.

The canoe is manned by a young South African couple—Terence Bell (24), a banned journalist and former 90-day detainee, and his 27-year-old schoolteacher wife from Johannesburg, Barbara.

The couple, due to start their journey at 4 p.m. yesterday, were delayed for more than an hour while Barbara telephoned to Johannesburg where her father, Mr. A. R. Edmunds, is seriously ill with heart trouble.

Just before their departure, Barbara told me that they would be facing the most dangerous part of their journey—the 22-mile Channel crossing—within about a fortnight.

CHANNEL RISK

Speaking in the Chiswick house where they have been living (the walls covered with A.N.C. posters and badges, anti-apartheid slogans and quotations from Lenin), she said: "We will take about five days to get to Dover from London.

"Crossing the Channel might be tricky—it is the farthest we will travel from land in the entire trip—but we will put up at Dover for a while and repack what little equipment we have as we wait for good weather to make the crossing."

Once safely across the Channel, the Bells intend travelling through France using canal routes. In the Mediterranean they intend keeping within two to three miles of the African coast—all the way round, through the Suez Canal and down to Dar es Salaam.

MARINES TELL

The Bells expect to take about two years to complete the trip. Terence Bell intends writing a book at the journey's end.

But no amount of chanting in the quiet English suburban atmosphere could disguise the fact that the small glass-fibre shell—which bears the A.N.C. name Amandhla (Strength) provided woefully inadequate protection.

On top of it all, the Royal Marines have warned the couple to look out for pirates and White slave traffickers along the Tangier coast.

Reports in the South African media about setting off (22 August 1967). Our parents were probably rather concerned.

had the outgoing tide in our favour. But soon that, too, changed. As evening fell, just beyond Blackfriars Bridge and the last photographer, we found ourselves stranded on a pile of rocks in midstream. We would have to wait for the tide to rise and, if not turn again, at least ease our paddling against it.

I suppose it was only then that it began to dawn on us what a

Farewell to Chiswick: setting off in calm water, having missed the peak of the tide

difference of up to seven metres (23 feet) between low and high tides really meant. Also, how long it takes for the tide to turn. It was this interval that allowed Joseph Conrad's narrator, Marlow, in "Heart of Darkness", to spin his African yarn.

We told no tales, but our mood was certainly "sombre" and "brooding" as night descended.

It was quite dark before we again pushed off into what was then a polluted waterway, especially where eddies swirled into dead water, leaving a residue of muck, oil and floating condoms. We were exhausted as we made our way through an eddy to reach a sloping stone bank beside the old coaling pier of the Blackwall Point power station at Greenwich. It was an awkward landing and we had to pull the kayak up the slope to the roadway at the top, lit by a solitary street lamp.

"Well, we've made it to Greenwich," I announced as we sat down to gather our breath.

"How do you know where we are?" asked Barbara.

Proudly, I showed her the map I carried.

"It's a bloody Michelin road map!" she exploded.

I quickly pointed out that the road map of the south of England *did* show the river and the places along its banks. We were in Greenwich and we knew about the old coal-fired power station.

"But it doesn't show where there are slipways or anything like that," Barbara complained as we struggled to fit the wheeled cradle under the kayak. "A road map! I don't believe it! A bloody road map!"

I had to admit she was right, but then I hadn't thought we would be under such pressure. And we had never, on our own, fitted the fully laden kayak onto the cradle, let alone pulled the craft up a stone bank. As we struggled to strap the kayak onto its wheels, Barbara kept muttering under her breath. I had to admit she had a point, but I kept my mouth shut as we finally wheeled the kayak off down the road toward a pub we had seen in the distance.

The pub had just closed when we knocked on the door, towing our oily, grime-encrusted kayak. We must have looked a sorry sight as the publican and his wife opened the door. We told them that we'd just come ashore after canoeing on the Thames. They peered at us rather incredulously, but they were sympathetic and let us put the kayak in their yard. We could sleep downstairs on the pub benches, they said.

Neither of us remembers much about that night except that the benches were red and that we lay down on them and didn't stir until early the next morning when the publican rushed in, newspaper in hand.

"You're the people that are going to Africa," he said excitedly, waving one of the mass circulation daily newspapers.

Oh hell, I thought, we've really done it this time. There would be no opportunity to stop, reflect, plan and prepare. No peace at all. We were going to have to brave this one out. At least Barbara was smiling.

"Yes," I said as confidently as I could, "this is our first stop."

In celebration of that fact we were given a free pub breakfast and waved off enthusiastically as we trundled *Amandla* back down the road to the river and the oily eddy by the old coal pier.

It was easier getting away, and the tide, although it had turned, was in our favour. The weather, at least, was marvellous: blue skies and only the lightest whiff of a breeze. We had successfully paddled out to catch the retreating tide in the middle of the river, when one of the many pleasure boats plying the region passed us. From the loudspeaker we heard, "And there you have the young couple who are paddling to Africa."

With no argument from Barbara, I turned back to follow a less conspicuous course close to the southern shore, reaching Greenhithe as the tide was turning.

We could see a slipway and a boathouse, so we headed in. It was the boathouse of the local Sea Scout troop and a couple of them were there to welcome us in. There would be no problem with us staying there, they said, and we could be away early as the high tide turned.

"Do you have a chart?" one of the sea scouts asked.

I waited in trepidation for Barbara to announce the embarrassing fact of the Michelin road map, but she didn't.

"Afraid not. Didn't have time to get one," I said.

"No problem," said the sea scout, "we've got some spares." And he presented us with a chart of the Thames estuary.

Indeed, the Thames was a river and it flowed into the sea. Neither of us had thought much about what that might mean. Even the sheer height of the tides hadn't prepared us for what we were about to confront: a distance of eight to ten kilometres — five miles and more — from one shore to the other before we would even reach the open sea.

CHAPTER 5

Sand, mud & the Thames estuary

Barbara had left details such as the phases of the moon and the tides up to me and, had I known what I was doing, I would have checked. As we set out from Greenhithe we paddled into a spring tide, when the difference between low and high tide is at its greatest. But at least we had a chart.

Poring over it after the sea scouts left, warning us about the dangers of tidal flows up the River Medway on the south side of the estuary, I plotted a course. We would paddle across to the north shore in the morning, where a long jetty was indicated protruding from Canvey Island. We would then relax as we waited for the tide to flow back in, before setting off diagonally across the estuary toward Whitstable, letting the tide take us "around the corner" and on toward Dover.

It all sounded quite professional and, as we moved downstream carried by the tide, the crossing toward the other shore went smoothly. But I had not expected the size of the swells we encountered. As we neared Canvey Island, with the tide having almost run its course into the sea, it was obvious we had a problem. The chart showed a long jetty, apparently sloping down to the low-water mark, but by the time we reached it, the tide was so low that the jetty stopped some ten metres short of the water.

"It's mud!" Barbara yelled as she stepped out, ankle-deep in a gritty sludge.

"It's okay. We'll have to pull the boat up to the jetty and take it to the top," I said as I stepped out into the ooze.

"Bugger you!" said Barbara and struggled toward the end of what was, in effect, a floating jetty. She pulled herself out of the mud, stepped onto the planks, and walked purposefully up the steep slope to the top. There she sat on the retaining wall, glaring down at me

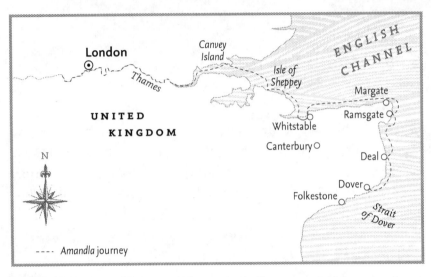

First lesson in inexperience: seven days to get to Dover

as I went through the painfully slow process of alternately pushing and dragging the kayak to the jetty, where I managed to manhandle it onto the platform at the end.

Although I was close to collapsing, I remember feeling proud that I had managed to succeed. My penance was done. At least, that seemed to be the way Barbara saw it. When I finally managed to get to the wall, she sympathised and apologised.

"But you got us into this in the first place," she noted for the record before we wandered off, hand in hand, to a local shop to buy two chocolate bars.

Sitting side by side on the retaining wall, we ate the chocolate and waited for the tide to lift the jetty. There was a breeze and the swells running into the estuary seemed even bigger than before. I had sudden thoughts of us being swept into the North Sea and out of sight of land, something I didn't share with Barbara. I knew I was being irrational. Although the swells were large and the current strong, the weather was clear and there was only a light breeze. As long as we could keep paddling through the heaving water in such a shallow draft vessel, we should be able to go with the tide and "zip around" to Dover, as

30

planned. In any event I had a compass, so we were unlikely to head off in the wrong direction.

But fear overcame rationality. I had already seen and done enough to realise how hopelessly inexperienced we were. Why gamble? In the most persuasive tone I could muster, I told Barbara that it was probably best if we followed the southern shore. We should get going before the tide was fully in and paddle diagonally in a south to south-easterly direction, across to the Isle of Sheppey, off the northern coast of Kent. We would have the advantage of a period of "dead water" before the tide fully turned. At worst we might end up further along the coast, but at least we'd be on the southern side.

As the tide was reaching its apex, we pushed off from the end of the Canvey Island jetty and headed south and east for Sheppey, referred to in ancient Saxon times as "Sceapige", meaning "Isle of Sheep". We would occasionally lose sight of the land ahead in the troughs and then glimpse it again as we crested another swell. We paddled as if our lives depended on it.

It was soon clear that we were not as fit as we should have been — our shoulders and backs ached. Nevertheless we ploughed on until landfall was clearly in sight. The water closer inshore was also calmer, but we had no time to appreciate this fact: just ahead of us were dozens of careening catamarans under full sail, skimming along, backwards and forwards, across the course we had set. As we drew closer we heard a loudspeaker from the shore, apparently squawking at us to "get out". We put our heads down and paddled frantically, trying as best we could to avoid collisions.

At last we ran ashore on what is locally referred to as a beach, but is, in fact, a bank of pebbles rather than a stretch of soft sand. And there in front of us was a small grandstand of spectators, come to watch what we later learned was an international catamaran competition. Fortunately we had not blundered into an even bigger set of international trials, which had taken place a few weeks before.

Accompanied by hostile glares and muttered comments, we pulled *Amandla* ashore, fitted the cradle and, somewhat sheepishly, left the scene, our hats pulled low.

"We'd better ask the locals about the best way to go," said Barbara as we set up our tent, a considerable distance from our embarrassing landing.

The nearby pub seemed a good place to make enquiries. After a meal of fish and chips bought at a local "chippy", we made our way to the pub, where we discovered that there were oyster beds along the coast of Sheppey. These should be avoided at all costs. We should also avoid being propelled by the inflowing tide up the Medway, the river that feeds into the Thames on the eastern shore of Sheppey.

By that time we had worked out the tides and felt we were becoming at least marginally accomplished paddlers. So we took on board the advice offered and prepared to set out the following morning as the tide was coming in.

After a good night's sleep we decamped and wheeled *Amandla* down to the water. The timing was perfect: the tide was still flowing out and the water looked calm. By keeping our eyes on the shore, we would avoid being swept up the Medway. Then, as the high tide turned, we would be in position to head briefly north and make our way beyond Whitstable, and "around the corner" towards Dover. With our hats set at jaunty angles, we set out.

Unfortunately, nobody had mentioned fog. We had no sooner pushed off from the shore than a mist rolled in, so thick that it seemed to cling to the sea and the sky, drawing down a gauzy curtain. It was impossible to know where we were heading.

Blindly we paddled, trying to keep within vague sight of the shoreline while checking the compass to make sure we were still heading east. That meant blundering through the oyster beds, grounding *Amandla* several times as the water retreated. We inched our way forward, with no idea where we would end up, although it would surely be south of Whitstable, up toward the River Medway. Finally, the water rose sufficiently and, on what we correctly assumed was the height of the tide, we made out the shore ahead of us, dead east.

We had obviously crossed the Medway, but how far upriver we hadn't a clue. Wherever we were, there was a level, grassy area ahead onto which we could pull *Amandla*. Perfect for camping.

Now, at last, we were properly on our way.

"I'm not cooking," said Barbara, as we finished pitching our tent.

On Sheppey, in addition to two bottles of beer, we had bought some bread, tomatoes and onions. Barbara fished out a tin of bully beef from the supplies and we had a dinner of bully beef sandwiches with sliced onion and tomato, washed down with the two bottles of beer. The leftovers would do for breakfast.

The next day we hoped to paddle our way, parallel to the shore, past Whitstable and Herne Bay to Margate, out of the estuary and on to Deal and Dover. Should the weather hold, as several fishermen on Sheppey had assured us it would, we could join a scheduled mass canoe crossing of the Channel in two days.

When we woke the next morning, the day was clear — the fog had lifted. But the high tide had already turned. Where water had been, lapping at the grassy bank on which we'd camped, lay an expanse of mud flats. We had obviously arrived at the height of the tide on the previous day. Now, not even an hour after the turn, there was nothing but primordial ooze.[1]

We made coffee, munched on the previous evening's leftovers and decided to portage to Whitstable rather than wait six hours or more in the hope of getting away in very shallow water. So we put *Amandla* onto its cradle and headed up to a road in the distance where we joined the bumper-to-bumper traffic of Britain's August bank holiday weekend.

It was a long, tiring haul, but we finally made it to the Whitstable

---

1 Barbara still insists it was sand, but we long ago agreed to differ.

harbour where, well into the afternoon, we deposited the kayak.

"It's safe here, but you can't stay," said the harbour official.

Obediently, we made our way up to a bed and breakfast establishment close by. Later I found some heavy tape and slipped back to the harbour to tape over the painted boast: "London to Dar es Salaam 1967". We could at least try to be incognito.

CHAPTER 6

Fog, a tidal surge & a nudist colony

With clear blue skies and little wind, we paddled out of Whitstable harbour on the morning of 26 August.

"We'll take it easy, camp at Broadstairs, leave early in the morning and be in Dover by nightfall," I announced confidently. There would be no more trouble with tides and we would stay quite close to the shore as we headed south. Inlets and bays would be of no consequence, since we would stick to a fairly straight line between 500 metres and a kilometre offshore, away from mud flats and other such obstacles.

We reached Broadstairs in good time and camped amid several sailing boats pulled up on the beach, among them former Prime Minister Ted Heath's *Morning Cloud*. At sunrise we pushed off and headed south, paddling steadily within sight of the shore. If there was any current, it seemed to be helping as we followed the coast toward Margate. It would be a long paddle — perhaps ten hours — to Dover.

But then that great curtain of fog came sweeping in again. Our Sea Scout chart had covered only the Thames estuary, so we headed in as close to the coastline as we could. The kayak almost collided with a couple of swimmers at one stage and we guessed we were close to Margate.

"That Michelin road map doesn't give a damn about the coastline and the sea," Barbara noted, as I stole a furtive glance at the unfolded map to check what came after Margate.

I hadn't thought we would need to know much about the coastline. Since our intended course was some way offshore, the ins and outs of the coast would be irrelevant.

They might have been, but for the fog. I trusted the compass, but didn't want to end up too far out to sea, so we kept on paddling close to the shore, often within sight — and usually sound — of what seemed like thousands of bank-holidaying Britons. Unknowingly, we headed through the murk into Pegwell Bay.

We were to find out later, in Dover, that Pegwell Bay is notorious for its extreme tides, sandbanks and bogs, and that it is home to the estuary of the River Stour. We discovered the sandbanks as we wallowed our way south, unprepared for the imminent practical lesson on tidal surges, those strong flows of tidal water that travel up shallow estuaries against the normal current.

As we paddled, poled and rocked to and fro to get off sandbanks, we suddenly found ourselves in deeper water and moving swiftly. I was ecstatic; as long as we weren't heading west and out to the open sea, we would be fine. An earlier glance at the compass had revealed that we were heading east and south as we picked up speed.

But then, as the fog lifted slightly, land appeared on the left. Impossible! England was surely to our right. And, to the left, across the Channel, surely France?

Through the mist we could make out sloping mud banks on which several launches were drawn up. There seemed to be a few men lolling on their foredecks, drinking.

In what I took to be my best British accent, I shouted across, "Excuse me, where are we?"

The answer came back immediately: "*Pardonnez moi?*"

This provoked great mirth among the drinkers, who were obviously aware of what had happened. Then one of them shouted, "You're up the River Stour, mate."

So we did an about-turn, still against the tidal surge, and headed back down one of England's great medieval waterways that had once linked Canterbury with the continent. It was very hard going, but we eventually made it out beyond the estuary and again into the maze of sandbanks.

The fog hadn't lifted and, with the constant rocking of the boat, Barbara started feeling seasick. It seemed we were getting nowhere until, through the mist, loomed the figure of a man, stark naked. In the swirling fog he seemed to be walking on air.

I greeted him with the same pathetic query: "Excuse me. Where are we?"

"Pegwell Bay Nudist Colony," he replied. "And where are you off to?"

Without thinking, I blurted out: "Dar es Salaam, Tanzania."

"Jolly good," he said, before pointing out, unnecessarily, that the immediate vicinity was extremely difficult to navigate. Then, telling us to "hang on", he seemed to melt into the mist before reappearing with another naked man, the two of them carrying a canoe and accompanied by a very buxom, naked woman who knelt in the front of their craft as they launched it, like the figurehead of some grand schooner. We followed them through the channels they were clearly familiar with, and away from the sand-clogged area.

"Straight on down to Deal and then to Dover," our guide said cheerily.

We thanked the nudist crew and headed off, exhausted. It was already late.

"We're not going to make Dover," Barbara said.

She was right. So we nosed the prow of the kayak into the pebbles of the beach at Deal in the early evening.

We set up our tent, ate the cold remnants of our readily edible supplies, made two cups of tea, crawled into our sleeping bags and slept until the early hours.

There was no time for breakfast as we quickly struck the tent and packed the kayak. Trying to reassure Barbara, I confidently announced that we might still make it to Dover in time for the canoe crossing. In any event, I assured her, as long as the weather held, there was bound to be another crossing we could join.

In my scant research I had read that swimmers and canoeists set out in calm seas, when the tide was coming in, paddling or swimming in a straight line with an escort boat. But they were then swept some

Handwritten note at top of postcard: Hi, folks, X (on other side)

Dover harbour: scene of a week of wet misery

twelve nautical miles up the Channel before being brought back by the retreating tide to land near Calais. But even my Michelin road map indicated it was unlikely that we could reach Dover in time, whether or not we paddled with the tide.

And so it was that *Amandla* and her intrepid crew paddled into Dover harbour on the afternoon of 28 August. Searching for a place to land, we noticed a concrete slipway leading up to the boathouse of the Royal Marines. Permission was granted and we set up camp in the military boathouse, only to hear that the weather was about to change for the worse. Fortunately, an Egyptian swimmer had arrived in Dover, keen to take on the Channel, and we were told that we could, at no cost, go along with his escort boat.

At least we would have time to put some of the necessary finishing touches to *Amandla*, we told ourselves. This included buying several more heavy-duty plastic chart cases to provide extra protection not only for our clothes and food, but also for what Barbara referred to disdainfully as "your office": my portable typewriter, a ream of paper,

38

carbon paper — so necessary for copies in the days before computers — and my rolls of film.

There can be few situations more depressing than being stuck in a chilly boathouse for days, listening to wind gusts rattling loose planks, doors and windows, rain pounding on the roof and icy waves crashing into the harbour. The town itself did nothing to raise our spirits and, apart from the occasional nodded greeting, most locals seemed as miserable as the weather.

But we bought in extra supplies and fitted runners along the bottom of the hull to protect against the abrasive sand and pebbles of beaches. Storage was also better organised and, without much enthusiasm, Barbara began exercising her culinary skills. The menu was limited largely to baked beans in various forms, eaten as we sat huddled around our paraffin stove. Here also began my almost daily ritual of typing up notes for inclusion in what I hoped would one day be a book about the voyage.

Two or three days after we'd arrived, a South African journalist tracked us down and interviewed us, reporting that we were waiting to cross the Channel. And wait we did. September brought no better weather. I was worried about winter in these northern climes and must have developed a rather optimistic image of "the Med". In my mind were not the tempests of legend that shipwrecked the likes of Odysseus, but a silly Cliff Richard song, "Summer Holiday", about bright sunshine and a blue sea.

It was Barbara who forced a decision. Her birthday was on 4 September and on 2 September she announced, "If this weather hasn't cleared by my birthday, I think we should take the ferry to France."

Reluctantly I agreed, hoping that in a couple of days the weather would clear, the Egyptian swimmer would be ready and we would paddle across. But the weather didn't oblige and my pleas for "one more day" were cut short.

"You agreed," Barbara said.

Indeed I had. And so we trundled *Amandla* out of the boathouse and down to the ferry terminal.

The crossing was uneventful, especially since nobody paid any attention to us or the trundled kayak. In Calais, still in stormy weather, we were directed to a local campsite near the city's yacht club. From this vantage point we could look across a heaving, slate-grey, white-flecked sea. The wind, as Barbara noted in a postcard sent to her parents, "makes Cape Town look sick". We had problems setting up the tent, but eventually managed it.

It was filthy weather for days and, when not huddled in the tent, we walked the damp streets of Calais. We did not find a market, but bought some more stores in the local supermarket and deli, not knowing what the next few days held in store. There were always the emergency rations if we were desperate. At least the people seemed friendlier than their counterparts across the Channel. We regularly had to doff our hats in response to a greeting as we strolled about. And, of course, there were the boulangeries[2] and patisseries[3] to cheer us up.

After a brief search we also managed to buy the most up-to-date available *fluviacarte*: a 1962 map of the navigable waterways of France. No more road map errors would be made and waterways were waterways. What could change? Especially when many dated back hundreds of years.

By torch or candlelight — our "*bougie*[4] power" — we pored over the chart as rain continued to drum on the flysheet of the tent. From Calais and into the Canal d'Aire we could enter a navigable system that could take us to Belgium, the Netherlands and Germany as well as to Paris and down to the Mediterranean.

I had a keen interest in the battles of World War I, among them

---

2   bakeries
3   confectioners
4   "Bougie" means "candle" in French.

the senseless bloodletting referred to as the Hundred Days Offensive of 1918. Along our route were names remindful of those ghastly four years when most of the world went to war for the first time: Somme, Marne, du Nord. However, the Canal du Nord, fought over at horrendous cost in 1918, did not seem to feature on our chart.

Part of the route we would paddle through was the coal-mining region, the territory of Émile Zola's literary masterpiece, *Germinal*, with its echoes of the idealism of the French Revolution. Here, a century before the Seamen's Strike in Britain, miners — men and women — had downed tools and suffered in the cause of a better, saner world. We would be travelling through history, both bloody and inspiring.

It was a romantic view, but at least we had covered the practical necessities. We could find our way with our chart while camping, cooking, travelling and living along some of the most historic waterways of northern France. Unfortunately, there was no mention of how long it could take to pass through a lock, going either uphill or down, to link with a higher- or lower-level waterway. Moreover, some of the canals, still in regular use, dated back to the seventeenth century, so we were unsure of the conditions we would encounter.

But we were keen to get going. Quite apart from anything else, France in 1967 was more expensive than England. We needed to be frugal with the £50 each the British government had allowed us for our travels. It was time to get on, away from the temptation of the nearby patisseries and the cost of the campsite.

As we mapped out our route along the waterways, we noted numerous small tick marks on the chart. But we paid no attention to them. Having secured our *carnet de passage*, the piece of paper that gave "pleasure boats" free passage through the locks of France, we began to feel that we were finally on our way.

We had also established what turned out to be a fruitful relationship with the postal service, which started with the assistance of the bank in London where we had deposited our savings. When we left

England, we asked the bank branch manager — such approachable individuals in authority existed in those days — if he would mind forwarding to Calais any mail addressed to us. We would use the bank as a forwarding address.

"No problem," he had said.

When we got to Calais, there was indeed mail waiting for us at the local post office. This was the *poste restante* service. The postmaster informed us that mail would be held for up to three months, "perhaps, even a year". If not collected, it would then be returned to the sender. If a forwarding address had been given, it would immediately be forwarded.[5]

Everything was now in hand. All we needed was a halfway decent day to set off down the Pas-de-Calais, bound for Paris, just 220 kilometres away "as the crow flies".

We had by now adjusted to our new way of life: sleeping on the ground in a two-person tent, cooking on a single burner, usually in a single pot, and washing in a small quantity of — at best, luke warm — water. It was very basic, but it provided an exhilarating sense of freedom.

---

5   The *poste restante* service is still in limited existence today, but usually at a cost. It was relatively free in 1967.

CHAPTER 7

Incognito into the French canal system

It was the silence that struck us first. After nights in a tent buffeted by wind and drummed on by rain squalls, it was suddenly eerily quiet. As I stuck my head out of the tent flap, the early morning sky was cloudless and everything smelled fresh. Barbara followed me as I scrambled out to get a view of the sea. I could make out the smudge that was England across mirror-like water.

"Just a few more days," I remonstrated, "and we could almost have walked across."

Barbara was unmoved. "But we're here, so let's get going," she said, with a clattering of pots and pans.

Much of what we had, including the tent, was still wet. We'd have to allow everything to dry before packing up.

It was late morning by the time we started loading *Amandla*. We were almost ready to set off when a young French couple approached. They greeted us, explaining that they were journalists. Were we the South African couple paddling to Dar es Salaam? they asked.

I don't think Barbara and I even exchanged glances before answering that we most definitely were not. I think we both felt embarrassed that we had not paddled across the Channel. Thankfully the words "London to Dar es Salaam" on the hull were still taped over.

The journalists thanked us and left as we wheeled the kayak down to the harbour.

Even in those pre-internet days, news travelled fast. Later that day, a South African newspaper announced that the Dar es Salaam-bound canoe couple were "lost in the Channel". Perhaps the Egyptian swimmer had finally set out, and had noted our absence on what was an ideal crossing day.

It must have been a shock to our families to see the news report.

S.A. CANOE COUPLE DISAPPEAR

From Our Correspondent
London, Thursday.

SOUTH AFRICA'S canoeing Bells — former 90-day detainee Terence and his wife, Barbara — have disappeared, but everyone associated with their London to Dar es Salaam canoe trip is certain there is a logical explanation and there is no suggestion of any mishap.

The Bells, who set out down the Thames in their 16½ft. canoe on August 21, were held up in Dover by bad weather for the past week.

It is thought that they may have decided to take a ferry across the Channel when the weather failed to clear.

Another suggestion is that they may have given up the venture and returned to London.

They had undertaken to inform journalists as soon as they knew for certain when they would be able to set out across the Channel.

No word was received so journalists visited the Royal Engineers' boathouse where they had been waiting but there was no sign of the Bells. Their canoe and equipment had been removed, and employees at the boathouse could offer no assistance as they had just come on duty.

Those who had been on duty while the Bells were staying at the boathouse have not yet been traced.

Another theory is that the Bells, who had exhausted the sights of Dover during their wait, decided to move on to another point on the coast before setting off for Europe.

Canoeing couple in France

From Our Correspondent

LONDON, Tuesday. — The mystery of the missing Bells — the two South African canoeists attempting to row from London to Dar es Salaam — has been solved.

Terence Bell, a former 90-day detainee and banned journalist, and his wife Barbara "disappeared" from Dover at the beginning of September.

In a letter reaching London from Paris today Mrs. Bell said they were due to start their journey down the French canals on Friday.

Several British newspapers also picked up on the story of our disappearance.

44

But only days later they received the postcards Barbara had posted when we arrived in Calais, telling them that we were fine, that the weather was lousy and that we were heading for Paris.

With our lifejackets wedged in behind us as backrests and our hats firmly on our heads, we were comfortable as we paddled steadily down the twenty-nine kilometres of the Pas-de-Calais to turn right into the Canal d'Aire. With no wind, currents or sandbanks to worry about, we seemed to speed along until we reached the first lock. Great big wooden doors provided entry to a basin that either raised or lowered the vessels in it, releasing them through similar doors at the far end.

It was then that we discovered that *Amandla* hardly qualified as a waterway priority. Certainly not in locks that handled 250-ton steel barges and pleasure craft that were like large apartments on the water. The lock-keeper quickly made it clear to us that unless we were lucky enough to get to a lock already quite full with larger craft, we would have lengthy waits as other, bigger, craft pulled in.

Fortunately, perhaps because it was so late in the year, we only had to contend with working barges. We were sent to the rear of the lock, the keeper apparently fearful that we might be run over by the steel monsters as they exited. But the back of the lock was a terrifying experience as the barges ahead started their engines and their propellers churned the water, pushing our small craft against the lock gates. We coped by hanging onto the gates, *Amandla* broadside, as the water churned around us. In time we would become quite adept at this.

After navigating the first lock we also realised what those little tick marks on the canal map meant — locks, locks and more locks. It was a rather daunting prospect. So when we reached the second, at Saint-Omer, we decided to camp. It was a fortunate choice because when we wandered into town the next morning, it was Saturday — market day.[6] There we topped up our supplies with rustic French fare before

---

6   We still take great delight in this French tradition.

COULEURS ET LUMIÈRE DE FRANCE

Next stop Paris? The start of the journey along the Calais canal system

tackling the next two locks, which we managed without mishap. Thereafter it was a long, calm stretch to the next lock, past Béthune.

Once out of the locks, the ancient canals tended to follow the lay of the land, and we would soon pass barges as they chugged along slowly so as not to damage the canal banks. These old canals meandered, making for leisurely, pleasurable cruising. Since the banks were almost level with the water, it was a constant sightseeing experience, even though we were so low in the water. Our only concern was that Paris was perhaps a great deal further by waterway than the 220 kilometres in a direct line. We began to worry about how long the journey to the French capital might take.

Our planned route to the River Oise (which links with the Seine at the aptly named Conflans) was elaborately decorated with ticks on the *fluviacarte*, both before Cambrai and beyond. The ticks were especially prolific beyond the town. I had hoped to camp or at least spend some

And so to the Rhône via canals and rivers

time in Cambrai since it gave its name to a World War I battle that saw the first major use of tanks. Artillery, aerial bombardment, infantry and armour combined to ensure a spectacular breakthrough of the German lines. This was short-lived, but proved that tanks were a part of modern warfare. Like so much else in this region, Cambrai also had a history going back at least to the Roman Empire. So much so that it features as the Roman camp of Compendium in the Asterix comic books.

But how long would it take us to get to, through and beyond Cambrai?

Our only consolation was that, because the town was on the River Escaut, this might be a busy route for barge traffic, with the locks in almost constant use. Hopefully most of it would be heading south and we could simply follow barges through the locks without too many delays.

There did seem to be a shorter way to reach the River Oise and, from there, the Seine and Paris. But according to the *fluviacarte*, this canal — labelled, as we recall, "St Louis" — was "under construction", I was only to discover later, when researching this book, that it was in fact the historic Canal du Nord, the one I had read so much about during my research on World War I battles. Reconstruction had begun in 1962, but since it was marked "under construction" we hadn't considered it. Nobody had told us that it had been opened to traffic in 1965.

However, as we approached what was on the chart merely a set of parallel dotted lines, we saw a barge emerging. The short cut was obviously no longer under construction. It existed. So we turned right off the Canal d'Aire and headed into uncharted territory. We were about to experience one of the most frightening episodes of our journey.

Once we had committed ourselves, there was no turning back, especially past the first lock. There was also nothing much to see apart from high concrete canal walls and sloping banks on either side of the wide waterway. It was like being in a giant bath. We weren't too bothered by this; it seemed worth sacrificing a view for the sake of speeding up our passage to Paris, our next mail stop. *Amandla* was moving faster than we could jog, let alone walk.

But then, in front of us, we saw a tunnel with a traffic light showing red. To the left were large wooden posts, obviously intended for vessels to tie up while waiting for the light to change.

There was nowhere to pull *Amandla* up a bank, so we drew up alongside one of the posts and waited. It wasn't long before we heard the steady drumming of a barge engine. Then, as the prow of the barge emerged from the tunnel, the drumming turned to a roar as the bargee opened up the throttle. We had never heard that sound before, since all the barges we had come across had been dutifully chugging along the ancient canals at little more than two kilometres an hour.

The roar was almost instantly accompanied by a bow wave that caught us completely unawares. *Amandla* was flung up against the post and toward the concrete wall. I fended off the wall with my paddle as the backwash almost tipped us over. Then I lunged for the post and managed to grab it with one hand, clutching my paddle tightly in the other as the water subsided. Fortunately, apart from a minor crack on one copper-tipped blade, the paddle was undamaged and so were we. Then the light changed to green.

"We can't go through there," said Barbara. "What happens if there's a barge coming?"

"That's why there's a light," I assured her as a tinny-sounding tannoy addressed us in French.

One word we clearly understood: "*Allez!*"[7] Whoever was yelling was obviously yelling at us and clearly wanted us to get going. So we did.

"Paddle like hell," I said as we sped into the tunnel.

There seemed to be posts sticking out of the sides of the canal walls at a height that could have knocked our hats off. I yelled to Barbara to keep her head down and, my hat jammed firmly on my head, chanted, "left, right, left, right," as we picked up the paddling pace.

---

7 "Hurry up!"

That was when the metallic voice seemed to grow frantic. There was obviously a loudspeaker system in the tunnel as well. Even if my French had been fluent, I doubt I would have been able to understand what was said. We were in panic mode and the sound seemed to echo in the dimly lit tunnel. We were paddling so fast that we set up our own small bow wave.

We were vaguely aware of areas where the waterway tunnel suddenly widened, obviously to allow vessels to pass one another. Perhaps there were other green and red lights, but we saw none. And the echoed screeching from the speaker system became increasingly frenzied. After what seemed hours, but was in fact less than thirty minutes, we burst into the sunlight on the other side and slumped in the cockpits, shattered.

It was then that we heard the splutter of an engine and a shouted French word that needed no translation: "*Merde!*"[8] A man was coming down the hillside towards us on a *tricycle mobylette*.[9] He shook his fist and uttered some more, fortunately unintelligible, words before heading into the tunnel on the towpath to manually move — as we later discovered — all the posts we had ducked under. These controlled the traffic through the tunnel, signalling, as each post was bent back, where a vessel was and in which direction it was heading.

"Let's get out of here," said Barbara.

I agreed. Somehow we found the strength to paddle briskly on, out of sight of the tunnel.

Near the junction of the old Canal de la Somme we found an area where we were able to camp. Neither of us remembers much of what happened after our nerve-wracking tunnel experience. Or even if we ate that night. We set up the tent, crawled in and slept soundly until just before dawn.

After we had packed up and stowed the tent securely behind my

---

8   "Shit!"
9   a three-wheeled moped popular in France at the time

cockpit, we pored over the waterways chart, preparing to confront the remaining locks.

"No more short cuts," said Barbara.

I assured her there was no chance of that. Only the "St Louis" section had been marked "under construction". What we had not known was that work on completing the Canal du Nord, fought over and badly damaged in 1918, had not started until 1960. Modern technology meant a deeper, wider waterway to allow faster, more efficient traffic and, instead of a series of locks up and down a hillside, a tunnel had been drilled through 4.35 kilometres of rock.

At least we had made up some time. But we desperately wanted to get back to the old canals or a wide river that would meander slowly through the countryside. We preferred the gentle etiquette of the older waterways, where bargees and their families would wave greetings and we would tip our hats in response. There the great steel craft posed no threat.

After several hours of steady paddling we reached lock number 17. It was a very deep lock and full of water at the time because the manually adjusted tunnel posts and lock-keepers upstream had signalled that a boat was coming through, headed for the River Oise. When we arrived the lock-keeper showed some surprise at the size of "Bateau[10] Amandla", but helped us to tie the kayak up alongside the lock. No reason to go any further, he assured us.

Like almost every lock-keeper we encountered, he was helpful and friendly, although somewhat puzzled by what we were doing in the waterway system with such a small craft. He introduced us to his family, said we should not bother to set up the tent, and insisted that we sleep in the basement of his house. Then, presenting us with a bag of apples, he said that he would see us off early in the morning.

That night, in the basement of the home of Éclusier 17, we joked about our stupidity in the subterranean passage of the Canal du

---

10 "Boat"

Nord and the wild reaction of the man responsible for the traffic flow. Then we tucked into a meal of stewed apples, cheese and bread, and collapsed into sleep before 9 p.m., still drained by the previous day's dramatic events.

It was barely daylight when the lock-keeper called out to us. But we were not only awake; we had washed up and packed away our kitchen.

"No more short cuts," Barbara repeated.

There would be none, I reassured her. No surprises. Only old canals and navigable rivers. Which was, of course, true. Except that navigable rivers are not all like the upper reaches of the Thames, our only experience so far.

And so, with *Amandla* looking smaller and more fragile than ever in the middle of the large lock, we waved farewell to the keeper. Then the water level dropped until the great grey doors opened and we paddled out, heading for the locks that would finally deposit us in the River Oise.

CHAPTER 8

In the wake of Robert Louis Stevenson

S hallow draft boats, probably not much bigger than our kayak, had plied the Oise since the Middle Ages, carrying people and produce between Paris and what later became the Netherlands and Belgium. As the mercantile age began, there was a need for more reliable waterways, not dependent on variable flows and shifting sandbanks. And so, from 1835, the Oise was tamed upriver by canals and locks.

Scottish author Robert Louis Stevenson was perhaps the first person to canoe down the Oise. In 1877 it was the locks around Cambrai that caused him such problems that he and his companion portaged their craft both by train and by cart to the lower reaches. As Stevenson wrote: "Fifty-five locks in a day's journey was pretty well tantamount to trudging the whole distance on foot, with the canoes upon our shoulders…"[11]

From Janville, where we exited the Canal du Nord, the Oise was still the river it had been for centuries. The flow was not very swift, but strong, making paddling much easier as we glided down to Compiègne. We were, at last, truly on our way. There would be locks, of course, but only a few until we reached Paris proper. Our arrival in the French capital would signal that London was well and truly behind us and we could set our sights on reaching Dar es Salaam.

Such romantic notions were probably stimulated by the weather: it was crisp, yet still warm, with autumn leaves along the river banks providing a mottled display of orange and red amid the green. And historic Compiègne, where we would allow ourselves an early stop, lay ahead.

I knew it was near here — at La Forêt — that the 1918 Armistice was signed, marking the Allies' victory over Germany and bringing an end

---

11 *An Inland Voyage, 1877*

to years of slaughter. Compiègne also featured in the extraordinary life of Joan of Arc, who was captured there in 1430. We might not be able to spend much time in Compiègne , but we could stop over briefly.

The first sign of the town was a local sports club along the river bank and we pulled up alongside. Several of the members on the grounds came over to greet us. At least one of them thought our venture crazy, but they welcomed us and not only gave us permission to camp, but to use the changing rooms too. Warm showers were an extraordinarily pleasant experience after damp rub-downs on canal banks.

Feeling clean and refreshed, we set up the tent and Barbara prepared a simple meal of bacon, mushrooms and eggs, with salad on the side. The *vin ordinaire*[12] we had bought in Saint-Omer went down extremely well. That evening at Compiègne we felt that life couldn't get better.

The next day was bright and sunny. After a riverside breakfast of fruit salad and cheese, we were sure we would quickly cover the near one hundred kilometres to the juncture of the Oise and the Seine at Conflans. Bolstered by our new-found, post-Canal du Nord confidence, we were sure that we could also make it to Paris within a day or two. We were convinced there would be mail waiting for us there; it would just be a matter of picking it up at our designated *poste restante* in the Parisian suburb of Saint-Denis.

As we headed downstream for Conflans, then the largest barge port in the country, I was sure all our travails were behind us. From now on, we would enjoy a steady but pleasant paddle down to the Mediterranean.

By then two weeks had passed since we had left England. We had not done too badly, we thought, given the delays caused by the locks. There would be more of them. But once we hit the Rhône, we would speed down to Avignon for a brief stopover before crossing the river

---

12 This is cheap table wine for everyday use – it went very well with meals such as Barbara's tomato and pepper stew described on page 193.

to the lock at Beaucaire. From there we would head into the coastal canal through the Camargue and then, finally, out to sea, to follow the coast to Spain.

Our naive hopes seemed borne out as we neared the great confluence: the Seine lay dead ahead. It was then that we noticed groups of men and women wading into the shallows, bags and nets in hand. They were scooping up fish. A number of large specimens were swimming close to the surface, apparently desperate to go back upriver. A sure sign of pollution.

"Looks like the Seine could be as bad as the Thames," I noted.

Although the water must have been poisonous to the fish, we discovered the following day that the Seine did not carry the debris and oily slick we had encountered coming out of London.

"If anyone offers us fish, we're not eating it," Barbara warned as we stopped over to camp at Conflans.

Instead, in celebration at having almost reached Paris in the two weeks we had set ourselves, we had pasta and a vegetarian stew washed down with the local *vin ordinaire*. Some of the local table wines were rough, but many were quite smooth and fruity, an excellent accompaniment to any meal. Our South African palates, accustomed to quite sweet "student plonk" or, at best, the imported Portuguese Mateus Rosé, had begun to adjust.

We decided that what we now thought of as a French lifestyle suited us well. While restaurant meals were out of the question, the wine was considerably cheaper than in England and, by shopping carefully in the delightful markets, it was possible to eat well on a very limited budget. Freshly baked baguette and a wide variety of local produce, ranging from cheeses to salamis, onions and garlic, were more than adequate to our needs. And our accommodation, apart from those days in the Calais campsite, had cost us nothing.

In our adopted Gallic mode, we breakfasted the next morning on milky coffee into which we dipped pieces of baguette. Fortified, we set

Turn left for Paris: Conflans, the confluence of the rivers Oise and Seine

out again, our confidence boosted by having covered the long distance from Compiègne to Conflans. We paddled strongly, accompanying — sometimes racing — barges headed up the Seine. Paris was at last within our reach.

Doffing our hats to waving barge families, we made our way into the great city, blissfully unaware that the suburb of Saint-Denis lies alongside the Seine, to the north of Paris, and that we had already passed it. We had heard of a camping area somewhat to the south of the great urban sprawl, situated right along the river bank in the Bois de Boulogne: a great, forested park that had once been the hunting ground of French kings.

Shortly after we had exited the last lock and were heading toward the area of the Bois, we noticed a small island, heavy with vegetation. Why pay to stay at an official campsite? We could camp on an island and come ashore during the day to pick up mail, buy what was needed, and do a little sightseeing. We were, after all, in Paris. Now we could have our own island to boot.

After pushing our way through reeds it was easy enough to land. The ground was firm and dry, with enough of a clearing to pitch our tent. We set up camp in the mellow light of the late afternoon, a stretch of water separating us from the parkland opposite, and settled in. Barbara began to prepare our evening meal while I took out my portable Olympia typewriter and recorded the events of the past few days. Only the clacking of the typewriter keys and the hiss of the paraffin stove disturbed the peace.

As night fell and the river traffic ceased, it became very still. The only sound was the gentle lapping of the water as we sat outside the tent, looking up at the starry sky. Here we were on our own island, with only a historic park separating us from one of the great capitals of the world. It was a magnificent feeling.

As usual, come morning we packed everything away, struck the tent and loaded the kayak. Then we paddled the short distance across to a small boatyard on the shore of the Bois de Boulogne. There we were given permission to leave *Amandla* and assured that all would be safe and secure. But when I asked about the post office at Saint-Denis, it emerged that it was a goodly distance away. In fact, a long walk and two metro rides away, right across the centre of Paris.

And so we set off on the first of several journeys from the Bois de Boulogne to the northern suburb of Saint-Denis, to find the post office. After getting lost and then taking the wrong metro train, we eventually found it — too late. At least we now knew where it was. But we had wasted the best part of the day, although we had managed to do some shopping for supplies.

I suggested that, next day, we shouldn't waste time by taking down the tent. It seemed quite well camouflaged. We would, in any event, have all our gear, supplies and anything of real value in the kayak. Early the following morning, we could fetch our mail, and do some shopping and sightseeing. The following day we could pack up and take a leisurely paddle through the famous city before heading south toward some of the old canals, to Briare and beyond. Consulting the waterway chart and doing some rough calculations, we agreed that our next *poste restante* — "Let's not make it any big town," Barbara insisted — would be Digoin, way down in the Loire Valley.

So it was that, right after an early breakfast, we stowed our bedding, office and kitchen and paddled across to the shore, leaving behind only our tent and torch. As we crossed over, we could still make out the shape of the tent on the island, but it seemed secure. Before heading across the city for Saint-Denis, we stopped at a café to belatedly celebrate our Parisian arrival with coffee and croissants.

This time we knew exactly how to get to the post office and, to make the journey worthwhile, there was mail. We sat side by side on a bench in Saint-Denis and read our letters. Barbara's family in particular seemed relieved that we were doing so well. Then, since it was still morning by the time we had finished, we headed off to the Place Pigalle.

Once before, in December 1965, when we had hitch-hiked into Paris en route to Morocco and were looking for a place to stay, we had been directed to a "young workers' hostel" near the Place Pigalle, at the foot of Montmartre, a hill to the north of the city centre. In my mistakenly romantic image of Paris I had assumed that Montmartre was on the left bank of the Seine because it was renowned for being the core of *la Bohème,* where the likes of Renoir, Picasso, Modigliani and Toulouse-Lautrec lived and worked.

But it turned out to be on the right bank and accorded with the somewhat seedy image I had from the musical "Irma la Douce", staged in Johannesburg in 1961. The hostel was down a side street, some distance from the square that is the Place Pigalle. It was incredibly cheap, clean, warm and very basic: two large dormitories (women on one floor, men on the other) with three-tiered metal bunks (no bedding provided), and communal ablutions with cold water only. Breakfast was a large bowl of hot, milky coffee and half a baguette.

Now, on our way back from the Saint-Denis post office, we couldn't find the hostel, but we climbed Montmartre for the first time. This was the site where the citizens of Paris and the National Guard started the revolt that became the short-lived Paris Commune. From 18 March to 28 May 1871, the revolutionary socialist Commune ruled Paris, refusing to accept the authority of the French government. The Paris Commune was to have a significant influence on the ideas of Karl Marx.

Later we managed to get to the famous Les Halles, the traditional central marketplace of Paris, to buy fresh food supplies. This was the setting of Zola's novel, *Le Ventre de Paris*,[13] his first to focus entirely on the French working class. In 1967 it was still the magnificent monument of cast iron and glass architecture (designed by Victor Baltard in the 1850s), which Zola would have known. Today it exists only as a metro stop and huge shopping mall.

Les Halles was the highlight of our market shopping en route. Parisian shoppers, almost certainly housewives, seemed to come not so much to buy as to investigate the produce. They prodded, sniffed and weighed by hand every fruit or vegetable before making a decision about a purchase. This was the mushroom season and there were many varieties available. None of the stallholders, in our experience, ever bellowed the French equivalent of the English "You bruise it; you buy it".

Late in the afternoon and filled with a sort of Gallic spirit, we made our way back to the Bois and boarded *Amandla*. I observed how well camouflaged the tent was: we couldn't see it at all from the boatyard. But as we got closer to the island, it was still disconcertingly invisible. And then the simple reason dawned — it was not there. Nor was the

---

13 "The Belly of Paris"

torch. Both had been stolen.

It was too late to go back to the boatyard to ask where we might be able to buy another tent, hopefully at a price that would not cripple us financially. We decided not to bother with another torch; candles and matches would do. Since I had learned bushcraft as a scout in my youth, I set about making a temporary shelter using branches, rope and groundsheets. At least our sleeping bags would not be drenched by condensation, sleeping so close to the water.

Barbara did her best to keep up our spirits by making mushroom-filled pancakes[14] with the supplies we had bought at Les Halles. But it was still depressing. We had no idea what another tent would cost and having to look for and buy one was almost certainly going to cost us another day.

We turned in early and the sun was barely up by the time we had dismantled our bivouac and started off for the shore and the boatyard. As we'd anticipated, it took most of the day to trudge about, find one or two camping shops and compare prices before buying — at a price in francs cheaper than our English tent — one that looked almost exactly the same.

"At least the weather's held," said Barbara.

The successful purchase of the tent and the clear, calm autumn weather seemed cause enough for celebration, so we stopped at a café for another coffee and croissant. We were back on the island that afternoon and Barbara seemed particularly happy with our new tent once we had pitched it.

Early the next day we set off. Paddling through calm, beautiful, historic Paris on that crisp autumn morning was extraordinary. Though brief, it remains one of the most enjoyable of all our travel experiences. Never to be forgotten.

And then, as we reached the outskirts, a reality check. A large family

---

14 Her recipe is on page 194.

were packing up their belongings from under a bridge where they had obviously been sleeping. It brought to mind the telling remark by the French poet Anatole France: "The law, in its majestic equality, forbids the rich as well as the poor to sleep under bridges, to beg in the streets, and to steal bread."[15]

The same inequality, only worse, applied in South Africa, with its particular racial twist. And it had led to resentment and mass resistance, something that appeared impossible in placid, well-ordered Paris, where even university students seemed to wear ties.

I began expostulating about the indulgence of enjoying a paddle through this city of the great Revolution of 1789, of the Commune of 1871. About the need to fight such iniquity in places where it was likely to happen. This, of course, just seven months before the student-initiated rebellion of May 1968 that saw President Charles de Gaulle flee Paris in the wake of the first nationwide general strike.

Barbara provided a second reality check by stating firmly, "*You* decided to go back to Africa by canoe."

That put paid to any more indulgent philosophical mutterings.

---

15 *The Red Lily,* 1894

CHAPTER 9

An anniversary dinner to remember

For couples who are still together after a year of marriage, a wedding anniversary tends to be a special day. And Barbara was determined that it would be one to remember, certainly in a culinary sense.

It was. But not in the way she had planned.

We set off from Paris on 25 September and estimated that we would be able to celebrate five days later in Briare. We should have looked more closely at the waterway chart and noted the number of locks we would need to negotiate to get there.

As we headed south, there were a number of barges going in the same direction. Having to share the locks with them, we were always ordered to the rear, even if we were the first to arrive. One of the barges was named *Hennie* and flew the flag of the Netherlands. For weeks, from the Seine and through the Loire Valley, we either tagged behind or raced *Hennie* between locks. The skipper, his wife and two children would come out of the rear cabin to greet us every time we came close. And we would observe the mother, almost every second day, hanging up or taking in washing from a line strung across the forward hold. In the locks we would also be given a warning signal from *Hennie*'s skipper when the gates were opening.

That signal meant it was time to cling onto whatever we could find against the back lock gates as the barge engines started up. There were eight locks on ninety-eight kilometres of the busy Hauts-de-Seine section from Paris and this gave us time to get accustomed to the experience of multiple propellers churning up water in our direction. After a while it ceased being frightening, but it was never pleasant.

We stopped over briefly at Melun on the Seine and Barbara bought most of the ingredients for our special anniversary meal: garlic, fresh herbs, olives, onions, carrots and rice. These we quickly stowed in the front of the kayak and continued on our way.

Finally, on 29 September, we made it into the Canal du Loing. Like several of the waterways of France, the Canal du Loing incorporates a river. Just under fifty kilometres long, it drops down thirty-seven metres and has a lock, on average, a little over every two kilometres. After forty years of digging and lock-building, this canal system had been open to traffic for more than three hundred years. The heavy wooden locks gates certainly bore signs of great age. We clung to these behind the sterns of barges and, despite the turbulence, the ancient canal, wandering through the countryside, was a relief after the busy Seine.

Once on the Canal du Loing, there was time to spare at the locks and Barbara managed to go ashore to one of the wonderful local markets to buy her final, and most important, ingredient — portions of fresh chicken. The poultry was handed over with the usual good-humoured banter.

By then we had realised that we were not going to make it to Briare for our anniversary. Moreover, our estimate of two weeks to reach Digoin was overly optimistic. There seemed to be an inordinate number of locks. In the fifty kilometres from the Seine to the delightful town of Montargis, there were nineteen locks. And then thirty-two more in the fifty-four kilometres to Briare. We had been able to cover the ninety-eight kilometres from Paris to the Canal du Loing in little more than two days largely because there were only eight locks. The Loire Valley canals were a different story. Patience was called for, along with the usual measure of physical strength.

On the afternoon of 30 September, somewhere between Nemours and Montargis, we pulled over to a bank. Since we were going to celebrate our first wedding anniversary with a special meal, I felt we needed one additional item — champagne. So I walked to a nearby town to seek out a bottle of — hopefully reasonably priced — bubbly.

To me, in those days, all sparkling wine meant champagne. Even the gas-infused, low-priced sparkling white wine in South Africa gloried in the champagne name. But, in that single excursion to a local wine store, I began to realise why the French might be rather touchy about this casual reference to the brand.

I asked for champagne and was directed to bottles in a price range way beyond my limited means. Seeing my difficulty, the owner introduced me to the *crémant*[16] of the Loire Valley.

"*C'est la même chose*,"[17] he insisted.

It was the same product, produced by the same "*méthode traditionelle*".[18] And the price was lower. That was how I received the first of several lessons about wine, its making and marketing, while gradually learning to appreciate the different types of fermented grape must and juice.

As the wine-store owner informed me, even if the same grape varieties were used, and the same methods were employed in producing the wine, it was only champagne if it came from the Champagne region. Yet champagne had become something of a generic term for the best sparkling wine, so it didn't take much to realise why that name was so jealously guarded. Or why the brand came at a premium price. In the event, I settled on one of the Loire *crémants* that didn't too badly dent our budget.

Then it was back to Barbara and *Amandla*, and a further paddle before tying up alongside a grassy bank to set up camp. It was a peaceful spot, seemingly in the middle of nowhere, although we could make out a village — possibly Nargis — a short distance away.

Barbara set about preparing her most ambitious meal to date: chicken cooked with carrots, onions and garlic, enhanced by the

---

16 A French sparkling wine
17 "It's the same thing."
18 "traditional method"

addition of olives, herbs and spices, and a goodly dash of left-over white wine. It would be served with rice, so she had two pots on the go, one for the rice and the other for what she decided to call "Chicken Anniversaire".[19] I noticed that she had even managed to buy some bay leaves for added flavour. Meanwhile I tied a string around the neck of the *crémant* bottle and sank it in the cold water of the canal to chill.

When she announced that the meal was just about ready, I pulled up the bottle, popped the cork and poured the wine into our mugs. We toasted our first official year together — and the *crémant* was very good. Barbara then dished up steaming plates of rice, which she topped with the chicken stew and gravy. It smelled sublime and I was ravenous.

I scooped up a forkful and blew on it to cool it. But when it landed in my mouth I froze. Seeing Barbara beaming proudly at me, I didn't want to spit it out, but my face must have registered that something was wrong.

"What's the matter?" she asked anxiously as I swallowed, grimacing.

"Just taste it," I said.

She did. And burst into tears. The paraffin supply, kept in the forward storage with the food, had leaked into the rice, and the stew, which she had carefully spiced and tasted throughout, had mingled with the grain and was ruined.

There was not much that could be rescued by trying to scoop off the bits of chicken, carrots, olives and other ingredients that had not been contaminated. We gave up and buried our great anniversary dinner.

Since it was still fairly early, I made my way to the village and managed to buy some cheese, salami and a loaf of bread. Only much later that night, having eaten our emergency meal and drunk the bottle of *crémant*, did Barbara see any humour in the situation.

---

19 "Anniversary Chicken" – the recipe is on page 195.

"But from now on the paraffin supply must be kept well away from the food store," she said.[20]

Next morning the weather held and we again caught up with *Hennie*. Our spirits lifted as we raced the Dutch barge to the next of several locks, where we would repeatedly be sent to the rear and have to wait. But at least we would soon be in Briare and could then make our way on to Digoin.

With winter approaching, we knew we had better get a move on. We had not only to get to Digoin, but then, by canal, with a multitude of locks, across to the River Saône at Chalon-sur-Saône. This waterway comprises the upper reaches of the mighty Rhône, then navigable by ships from the Mediterranean up to Lyon.

We did not think of the ships, only of the river that flowed south — strongly, we presumed. It would speed our paddling down to the Mediterranean. But we still had the Loire Valley ahead, starting at Briare, on its eastern edge.

---

20 Ever since then she has always tasted — or asked me to taste — cooked dishes before serving them.

CHAPTER 10

Aqueducts & terror on the Rhône

The town of Briare was famous for its navigable aqueduct. But we didn't know this until we got there. The waterways map had not revealed that we would have to cross the River Loire. If it had, we hadn't noticed. In fact, as we discovered only many years later, it was the longest waterway bridge in the world until 2003, when the Magdeburg Water Bridge in Germany was opened.

Coming across that aqueduct was another of those never-to-be-forgotten moments.

"What incredible engineering," Barbara remarked, reflecting her father's practical influence, as we looked out over this six-metre-wide, 662 metre-long trough of water with towpaths on either side.

Horses — and sometimes people — would have towed barges across this bridge when it first opened in 1896. Before then the canal we had just navigated ended at the River Loire and the Canal de Briare started on the other side. In times of drought there was too little water in the river to get across, while in the more frequent times of flood, it was extremely dangerous, if not impossible. And so the aqueduct was built, linking the Canal du Loing with the Canal de Briare. Although we had no way of knowing all the details, we felt we were part of this history.

We took considerably longer to cross the aqueduct than we needed to. It may seem silly, but sitting in a kayak on a water bridge high above the Loire Valley was exhilarating, and we wanted to make the most of it. Once across, we pulled our hats down tight and raced *Hennie* and any other barges in sight, trying to make up as much time as possible. Briare was an interesting town with a large yacht harbour, but we couldn't delay any longer.

It was a long haul to Digoin: nearly 200 kilometres with thirty-six locks that took craft up 41 metres (135 feet), then down 85 metres (279 feet). Fortunately, in a canal that opened to traffic in 1838, the water was almost level with the banks. This gave a panoramic view of the countryside: timeless, rustic scenes through which we often sped, paddling frantically. When a lock loomed, we would sit up, rest our paddles and coast toward the open or closed doors. Either way, we would have to wait outside until a barge turned up. Once in a while, a lock-keeper would allow us through on our own, a courtesy we always acknowledged with a deep doffing of our hats.

We also had some rain on the way down. But the occasional shower was not enough to dampen our spirits or make it difficult to set up camp, as in Calais. And we did make good time, at least by the standards we had now been forced to accept. Ah, would that we had been able to start earlier in the year.

The weather was mild with not a breath of wind as we steadily paddled towards Digoin, admiring the countryside. It was then that Barbara first spotted them: two wooden barges that could have come straight out of the nineteenth century, or even earlier.

We stopped paddling and glided by. As with the great steel barges, the rear of the vessels contained the living quarters while the front end was the hold for carrying goods. But these charming wooden craft were smaller than the diesel-powered modern boats. Moreover, in the middle there seemed to be another section: a stable with a sort of drawbridge door. This housed a horse that towed the barges along the towpaths, as other work horses had done over the centuries.

One of the bargees led his horse out along the towpath, hitched to the wooden craft. It was as if we had entered another time.

"I don't think we'll ever see something like that again," said Barbara, "except in a museum."

As we slipped past, I turned to get a last glimpse of the horse-drawn barge, and in the process knocked off some clothes drying on the kayak canopy. I reached out awkwardly to grab a pair of red underpants before they disappeared under the water — and then recoiled as a stabbing pain ripped through my chest.

"What's happened?" asked Barbara, looking anxiously back at me.

"Either it's cramp or I've pulled a muscle," I replied. "But I got the underpants."

It was small consolation to have salvaged some of my underwear. I found it unbearably difficult to paddle. Fortunately, we were almost at the aqueduct entrance to Digoin and it was soon obvious that the canal flowed right through the centre of the town. Perhaps we could find a place to pull up and I could get to see a doctor.

Then good fortune struck. Passing under a bridge, we noticed a quite large, triangular patch of grass alongside one of the bridge posts. We could tie up *Amandla* out of harm's way alongside the bank and pitch the tent under cover of the bridge — accommodation right in town. And it had taken us little more than a week to get there.

It was with some difficulty that we set up camp, because I found it painful to use my left arm. But we got the tent up and our kitchen neatly housed under the bridge. Using the paddles and a length of thin nylon rope, we also constructed a washing line and hung out the red underpants and other clothing to dry.

The following day we scrambled out and sought a doctor. He did a cursory examination, diagnosed a torn muscle, gave a prescription for painkillers, recommended "about ten days' rest" — and charged a considerable amount of money.

"We can't afford ten days," I lamented to an unresponsive Barbara, who had followed the doctor's instructions and put my left arm in a sling.

It seemed we would just have to wait. And as it turned out, that was not a bad thing. When we at last found the post office in Digoin, there was a generous pile of mail for us from both our families. Included was a note from Barbara's father saying that, after consulting an atlas, he had decided we meant Dijon, not Digoin, and had sent some mail

The second aqueduct: crossing into the town of Digoin

there. We explained this to the local postal authorities, who accepted this as perfectly normal, contacted Dijon and had the mail forwarded to us in Digoin.

In our encampment under the bridge, we replied to the letters and cards and, typing with one hand, I set about detailing everything that had happened to us on the way down from Briare. We were particularly keen to tell about the wooden, horse-drawn "Napoleonic barges" we had seen, so different from the luxury steel barges of modern times.

I also "took it easy" while Barbara experimented with new ways of preparing our meals. Digoin, as she noted in one of her postcards to her parents, was "heavily vegetarian".[21] By this she meant, not the town itself, but what we ate, largely determined by budget constraints.

Feeling quite proud of the distance we had travelled over the past

---

21 Some of her vegetarian recipes from this time are given on page 196.

two months, I bought a small can of paint and a brush and set about painting on the kayak the names of the various places we had passed through. I also resumed my written account of our adventures and edited several short stories I had drafted on the earlier trip to Morocco.

But time was pressing.

Then, in one of our rambles through Digoin, we discovered that a train ran almost straight across from Digoin to Mâcon, on the Saône, south of Chalon-sur-Saône. Barbara reminded me of my resistance to crossing the English Channel by ferry. Still, I saw this as different.

"It's a portage," I announced. "You are allowed to portage around difficult obstacles when you're canoeing."

That, after all, was what Robert Louis Stevenson had done on the River Oise, back in 1877.

The difficult obstacles in this case were the sixty-one locks, let alone the 112 kilometres of the Canal du Centre.

After a week my chest was better, so we wheeled *Amandla* to the railway station and, with the aid of the guard, put the kayak (labelled "to be collected in Mâcon") into the luggage compartment of the train. Then we headed out onto the road to hitch-hike to Mâcon. It took just three hours for a journey that by canal might have taken two or three days. We had, in the meantime, given as our forwarding *poste restante* address the post office in the town of Vienne, some thirty kilometres south of Lyon. Although we thought we might travel faster on the rivers, we were taking no chances.

In Mâcon we found a truck driver who, for a very small "contribution", brought the kayak from the station to the campsite adjoining the river where we had based ourselves. We looked on gleefully as the kayak was unloaded beside the River Saône, which flowed strongly and steadily southward.

The next morning, early, we were on our way.

Our only regret was that, because of time pressure, we were going to miss Lyon. I had wanted to stop in this city not only because it was where the Lumière brothers had pioneered movies, but also because it was the scene of the great silk workers' rebellions of the nineteenth century. The first rebellion, in 1831, was over cuts in wages and is credited as being the first of the worker uprisings of the Industrial Revolution. It was also the first time that workers managed — briefly — to seize control of a city.

To make up for missing Lyon, I told Barbara that we would stop over for "perhaps a day or two" in Avignon, not only to "catch our breath" before the final move into the sea, but to savour the area where my mother's Huguenot forebears originated.

We swept past Lyon on water that flowed at a speed of several metres per second (according to some), to the confluence of the rivers Saône and Rhône south of the old city. By our estimate, proudly conveyed in a postcard home, we were capable of moving at more than ten kilometres an hour, even if we were taking it easy. This was, to us, very impressive. The faster, the better, we thought. We reckoned we would be in the Mediterranean in no time.

But our speedy progress also meant that we needed an inlet or a cove that provided an eddy, a circular current to the main stream, in order to land safely. As we approached Vienne, a town that features prominently in the history of the Crusades, the Knights Templar and pilgrims of old, we spotted one and made for the shore. One of Barbara's shoes that had been drying on the kayak's canopy fell into the water and sank. But we made it, although we were a few kilometres outside the town.

I joked that it was perhaps appropriate that Barbara, with her Christian background, should have to hobble, barefoot, along gritty pathways into Crusader territory.

She sighed, rolled her eyes and noted, as she has many times since, "You have a most peculiar sense of humour."

My reference to the Knights Templar was at least accurate. It was in Vienne that Pope Clement abolished this Crusader order, although the mythology lives on not only in the eighteenth century novel *Ivanhoe*, by Walter Scott, but also in various Masonic orders.

Barbara, a high school Latin scholar who had read the Gallic wars of Julius Caesar, had her own reasons for wanting to see Vienne. The town has a history dating back more than 2,000 years, when it was a provincial Roman capital and important urban centre called Vienna. She was keen to see some of the town's Roman ruins.

Unfortunately, being in a hurry, we weren't able to do much exploring. After buying Barbara another pair of shoes in town, we found the post office and picked up our mail, giving our forwarding address as Sète. This is about a hundred kilometres west of the Rhône, along the Beaucaire branch canal that links with the coastal waterway system and — perhaps the greatest waterway feat of all time — the Canal du Midi.

We had been estimating two weeks between *poste restante* offices, and thought we should easily make it to Sète by then, even if we spent a day or two in Avignon. So we made our way back to the river bank where we had tethered *Amandla* and prepared to depart. We had every expectation of simple, speedy progress.

What we knew, but never seriously considered, was that, in those days before the Rhône was tamed by canals, it was a fully navigable river, with ships and barges plying the more than 300-kilometre route between Lyon and Port-Saint-Louis-du-Rhône, where the river empties into the Mediterranean west of Marseilles. Only at Baix was there a lock in a huge weir that provided hydro-electricity to the national grid.

We knew that there might be ships and barges. But we knew nothing about the effect on the river of ships with a displacement of hundreds of tons coming upstream. All we had been told when we left Mâcon was that we should give way to vessels coming towards us; a kayak would have no right of way.

Once on the water we soon hit a problem: a large cargo ship was coming upriver. We seemed to be hurtling toward its prow as two sharp blasts were sounded on the ship's siren.

I dug a paddle blade in, turning the kayak toward the shore, and began to paddle desperately, forgetting about any damage to my recently torn muscle. *Amandla* was broadside to the advancing ship, being pushed by the current faster than we could paddle toward the shore — except that Barbara wasn't paddling. She was transfixed, staring at the looming prow of the ship.

"Paddle, dammit!" I screamed.

Looking startled, she began to paddle frantically. We seemed to shoot past on the ship's bow wave and then we were tossed about like a cork, as the waves caused by the ship's displacement met at the stern of the vessel before flushing back to the river banks. Somehow we managed to stay upright.

"Paddle, dammit!" I yelled again as Barbara sat bolt upright in front of me, her arms rigid and her hat, held by the chin strap around her neck, hanging limply down her back.

And then, suddenly, it was over. The river was once again calm, though still flowing strongly. At least we now knew what to expect.

We cautiously steered a course closer to the shore. Fortunately not too close. Several barges, lashed together to give them more power against the current, made their way upstream; we were able to turn *Amandla* into the returning wave, after narrowly avoiding being grounded by the retreating water.

As we continued steadily toward Baix I tried to lighten the mood, telling Barbara that I had finally hit on a title for the book I was writing about our trip: "Paddle, Dammit!"

She was not amused. Anyway, as we reached the weir at Baix we soon had other problems to contend with.

CHAPTER 11

Avignon, a water rat & rosé

The little village of Baix doesn't even appear on the modern *fluviacartes* because the new, navigable, canalised waterways bypass it. But it still plays its part in harnessing the power of the Rhône to provide electricity. The small islands in the river made it, in ancient times, a perfect place for crossing from one side to the other. The Phoenicians settled there, as did the Romans, and the village was sacked by both the Vandals and the Saracens.

We got to know quite a bit about Baix because we were stranded there by the weather. After we struck the barrage and took three hours to portage across, storm clouds gathered and the first drops of rain began to fall. We managed to set up camp in an open field near the town before the storm really hit, rain pelting down amid strong gusts of wind. There was no way we were going to tackle the Rhône in such inhospitable conditions. And so, quite pleasantly, we decided to wait out the weather in Baix.

We battened everything down as well as we could, and in our waterproof orange anoraks, with our hats wedged in under our hoods, we became acquainted with the village, some of its perhaps six hundred inhabitants and its rather good white wine.

Nobody expressed surprise at the fact that we had arrived by kayak. We felt quite at home.

After a couple of days the weather cleared and we set off again, riding an even faster current toward Avignon.

"We're going like a rocket," Barbara said with renewed enthusiasm.

I knew I'd been forgiven. We were certainly travelling faster than we had ever done before. Later we were told that the river had reached speeds of thirteen kilometres an hour. We could believe it.

Then, ahead of us, we saw the famous fifteenth-century broken bridge of Avignon.

"*Sur le pont d'Avignon*,"[22] I bellowed out as we scanned the left bank for an eddy that would allow us to stop and get ashore.

But we were travelling too fast. By the time we noticed a potential landing place amid the walls and steps on the bank, we had already swept beyond it. And there was no way we could fight back against the current. In minutes, the ancient city was behind us.

We pulled in as close to the shore as we could until we struck some shallows and were able to beach *Amandla*. Landing, we pulled the kayak up over an area of muddy reeds and tree roots, before finding a clearing where we set up camp. We were keen to walk to Avignon, but it was a great deal further than we had first thought and there was no way we could get the kayak back upriver.

The excursion to Avignon was a minor disaster. We were too footsore and weary to appreciate even the great market that I had read about and wanted so badly to explore.

We bought a few supplies and then, as we turned to trudge back to our camp, Barbara said bluntly, "Sod Avignon. Let's just get across to Beaucaire."

I, too, had lost my enthusiasm for Avignon. Beaucaire, on the opposite side of the river, some thirty kilometres south of the medieval city, was entered via a lock, and there would have to be an eddy, or an inlet with dead water, into which we could safely glide.

So, early the next morning, we carefully looked left and right for any other traffic, then paddled directly for the opposite shore. Like in the North Sea and the Channel, the current carried us several kilometres downstream before we changed course to paddle with it.

We turned into the Beaucaire lock in about two hours. The great wooden gates were open and we paddled in, calling out to the lock-

---

22 "Sur le pont d'Avignon" ("On the Bridge of Avignon") is a French song dating back to the fifteenth century.

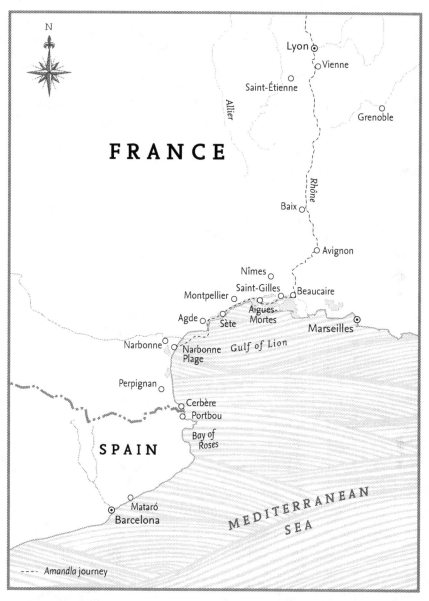

By river to the Mediterranean Sea

keeper, since there was no way out of the wooden-walled container.

There was no response.

We waited.

From time to time we called out again and waited some more.

Finally, the lock-keeper appeared at the side of the lock, metres above us, leaned over and told us we would have to wait. A *péniche*[23] might be along at any time, he said.

It was then that we noticed something in the water, swimming toward the prow of the kayak.

It was a rat. A very large water rat. As it reached *Amandla*, it started scrabbling to get onto the deck. We couldn't tell where it came from, but it had decided to board.

"Hit it," I instructed Barbara, who was gently pushing the rat away from the kayak every time it tried to scramble onto the decking.

"But it'll drown," she said.

She finally conceded that it was us or the rat; we could not allow the rodent aboard. After much splashing and shouting, the rat, by then probably badly battered, swam away out of the lock, toward the Rhône.

It was past midday when the lock-keeper finally relented. Perhaps it was because he had heard — and possibly seen — our desperate battle with the water rat that, like us, seemed to have no way out of the lock.

Then the gates started closing, the water rose, and us with it. The inland gates opened and we were on our way, through one more lock, paddling strongly to cover the approximately twenty kilometres to Saint Gilles.

We hadn't intended to stop at this town, but having spent the best part of the day trapped inside an ancient lock with a rat, we felt it would be therapeutic. So, on reaching Saint Gilles, *Amandla* was tied to the bank and we strolled up to the village square.

---

23 barge

The weather was warm, sunny and windless. Time to find a little café.

Everything was silent. It was the south of France and, even with winter approaching, siesta was still observed. However, outside a café there were some tables and chairs, one of them occupied by a well-dressed older man with a camera on the table before him.

We greeted him in French. He responded in English and invited us to sit down, introducing himself as a writer who specialised in architecture. He was in Saint Gilles to write about Romanesque architecture — "the style, not by the Romans," he explained. He was fascinated that we had canoed from London and said he welcomed the chance to improve his (already quite impeccable) English.

When he heard that we were looking for drinks and a bite to eat, he told us that he knew the *"patron"*[24] and, although it was siesta time, he could arrange something.

He did — delicious bread, cheese, olives and paté.

Our new friend was not surprised that we knew nothing of the famous Benedictine abbey in Saint Gilles, but appalled that we did not know about the region's famous rosé wines. Although it was getting on in the afternoon, it was still warm, and frosted glasses of rosé were duly delivered, along with a fascinating history about the wine and the area.

Rosé, he said, was originally made only for popes and kings. It was the true *"grand vin"*.[25] And he considered the rosés of Saint Gilles to be among the finest anywhere. I had always considered rosé to be merely red and white wine "chucked together", although I put this opinion to him rather more delicately.

And so, while savouring the second or third local vintage, Barbara and I discovered that, properly made, rosé comes from red grapes where

---

24 "proprietor"
25 "great wine"

the juice is only in temporary contact with the skins. An alternative method is by "*saignée*": "bleeding" some juice off vats of freshly pressed black grapes — the "must".

Several glasses later we agreed that not only were rosé wines "*très bons*",[26] but there were subtle differences in flavours, apparently depending on the cultivars used.

We also heard about a beautiful Romanesque portal at the abbey and about the shrine in the crypt, visited by women pilgrims who wished to become pregnant.

That was not the only reason we decided we should not stay longer. By that time it was nearly evening and our friend was heading back to Paris. We still had a long — more than seventy-kilometre — paddle to Sète. But since it was almost sunset, we thought we should camp somewhere along the way. Barbara suggested a light dinner of savoury scrambled eggs.[27]

After wishing one another "bon voyage", Barbara and I strolled back to the canal.

I suggested we paddle a few kilometres before setting up camp. But the rocking of the kayak was too much for Barbara.

"I'm getting seasick," she announced after only a few hundred metres, so we pulled in to the shore.

"Too much rosé," she said.

I set up the tent and she crawled in with her sleeping bag.

"If you want dinner, you can make it," she said.

I didn't, and we were both asleep shortly after nightfall.

We woke up bright and early, got coffee going and boiled a couple of eggs. Sète by afternoon, we vowed.

We didn't make it. Barely twenty kilometres further on, we came across something we couldn't at first believe was real. The walled

---

26 "very good"
27 The recipe for these is on page 198.

medieval city of Aigues-Mortes was like something out of a Cecil B. deMille movie epic.

We knew that the Crusaders had set sail from places such as these, eight hundred and more years ago, to claim the "Holy Land" as the true home of Christians. But we never expected that anything like this had been preserved. There wasn't even a sign of a television aerial poking up above the battlements — a fact enforced by municipal regulation, as we subsequently discovered. We simply had to stop here, even if only for a day or two.

A short branch canal housed a small harbour alongside the city walls. Beyond this lay large saline beds where salt was mined, as it most likely had been since the later part of the Stone Age. This, no doubt, gave the name to the area and, later, the town — Aigues-Mortes, meaning "dead water".

The canal then made its way to the sea, to the Grau-du-Roi, the "pond of the king". It was down this canal and into the "pond" of the Mediterranean that King — later Saint — Louis IX and his Crusader army had sailed in 1248 and again in 1270 on the seventh and eighth Crusades.

There were two vessels that caught our eye as we paddled, awestruck, toward the moorings at Aigues-Mortes: a beautiful wooden motorised yacht, *Wanderbird*, and a sleek, modern fibreglass vessel, *Shalimar*. Both were to play a significant part in our lives in the weeks to come.

CHAPTER 12

Aigues-Mortes & a Vietnam lesson

After tying *Amandla* up alongside the bank of the small harbour at Aigues-Mortes, we strolled beside the towering grey walls of the town. It was difficult not to fantasise about walking in the footsteps of medieval knights, merchants, peasants and, no doubt, slaves. But we had more prosaic matters in mind — primarily, where to stay.

We agreed that we should try to get permission to camp in a sheltered spot beside these ancient walls. So we walked around until we found what seemed like a perfect spot, grassed and protected from the wind by a protruding battlement. But whom to ask for permission?

A citizen of the town informed us that the official we should see was a good man and member of the PCF — the French Communist Party. Aigues-Mortes, our helpful citizen explained proudly, was part of the "Red South", although there had been something of an upset lately, with an independent republican becoming mayor. He directed us to the municipal offices, where we were cordially greeted by the PCF official and introduced to the mayor himself. He heard us out and granted permission for our *petit*[28] encampment beside the great walls.

Back at the harbour, when we went to fetch our tent, bedding and kitchen, we found that *Amandla* had attracted the attention of the occupants of *Wanderbird* and *Shalimar*: a retired English couple, Bill and Muriel Kerr, and a Belgian artist, Marc, and his wife. Bill and Muriel, jovial Londoners, invited us aboard. They told us that when Bill retired from his work as a printer in London they had sold their house and car and bought the motorised yacht, intending to spend their twilight years cruising the Mediterranean.

While we were speaking to the Kerrs we were joined by Marc.

---

28 small

PAR AVION

Crusader walls of Aigues-Mortes and the Tour de Constance. View from the harbour

After hearing about our paddling venture, he had a proposition. He intended to sail to the Caribbean with his wife before Christmas, returning for the summer. He needed crew. Would we like to come? We could either leave *Amandla* in Aigues-Mortes or transport her on *Shalimar*'s deck to and from the Caribbean.

While Marc's wife appeared frail and wore a constant look of fear, Marc was tall and strongly built and we didn't for a moment doubt his sailing credentials. So we were tempted, but turned down the offer. The weather had so far been reasonably pleasant, but it was a matter of time before winter really set in. I had another of my blind convictions: if we could be south of Barcelona by the end of December, the weather would be warmer. Somehow that seemed all that mattered.

Over the next couple of days we explored the ancient town, discovering that the great Charlemagne had first built a fortress here more than 1,000 years ago. A childhood memory stirred when

I was told that the circular building outside the city walls was the Tour de Constance (Tower of Constance). During the seventeenth century persecution of the Calvinist Protestant minority known as the Huguenots, this became a prison for a group of devout Protestant women who refused to renounce their faith.

My mother's family had fled this region of France, arriving in South Africa in 1688. The Edict of Nantes, signed in April 1598 by King Henry IV of France, had given the Huguenots the right to practise their religion without fear of persecution. The revocation of the Edict by King Louis XIV in 1685 meant that they were regarded as heretics and brutally persecuted. I knew of the Edict of Fontainebleau, which revoked the Edict of Nantes, and I knew of the tower, though not of the town.

Now inside those imposing grey walls was a thriving little village with bars, restaurants, a boulangerie and a superb patisserie. There was also an imposing Crusader church where one could imagine knights of old kneeling before the altar with heads bowed and hands clenched over the hilts of broadswords, swearing to liberate the holy land for Christendom.

We were sad to leave, but warmer climes beckoned. So, on an overcast day in late November, after a very pleasant stay of several days in Aigues-Mortes, we paddled away from the battlements and the Tour de Constance, and turned left into the Canal du Rhône à Sète.

We hadn't been paddling for more than an hour when a cold wind picked up and the first icy drizzle began.

"Paddle faster. It'll keep you warm," I advised Barbara, who retorted with a single expletive that dismissed my advice.

It was miserable as we paddled through the town of Palavas-les-Flots and stopped at a campsite on the outskirts. During a brief let-up in the drizzle, I pitched the tent.

"I'm not cooking in this," said Barbara, so we decided that I should paddle back into town and pick up supplies for a ready-made supper.

I had stopped beside the canal wall in Palavas when I was greeted in English by a tall American with curly red hair. He introduced himself as Denny, or "Den", Frank and wanted to know what on earth I was doing in Palavas in a kayak. I told him our story very briefly and mentioned that I was in town to pick up some supplies for our evening meal.

Denny immediately insisted that we leave the campsite and move into his apartment for a day or two, or at least until the weather cleared. He was sure his wife, Bonnie, would welcome the company. So we left the tent and kayak in the care of the campsite authorities and moved in with the Franks.

We discovered that Denny, a New Yorker of Italian ancestry, had dodged the draft by being accepted as a medical student at the University of Montpellier. During the long summer vacation, he and his wife, a slim, dark-haired New Yorker of Jewish background, would return to work in the United States to pay for tuition in France — a free pass from the draft.

While we were staying with the Franks, an "old buddy" of Denny's from New York arrived, having completed a long tour of duty in Vietnam. His name was Danny. In the two-roomed apartment, Denny and Bonnie slept in their bedroom, Barbara and I shared a camp bed and Danny slept on the couch.

Den, Bonnie, Barbara and I got on well from the start, but Danny seemed unable to make contact. Morose, withdrawn and "twitchy", he refused to talk about his experiences, admitting, when pressed, only that "it was awful".

We, great anti-war warriors, thought we knew all about how awful war was. We knew about the napalm, the carpet bombing and the massacre of poor Asian peasants on the orders of imperial Washington. We were proud to be part of the anti-war movement, holding the moral high ground against this mindless slaughter. While we pontificated, Danny sat in the corner, silent and ill at ease. With hindsight, he was obviously suffering from severe post-traumatic stress.

The following day, when Denny and Bonnie had left to go up to Montpellier, I had a chance to speak to Danny alone. He wasn't very communicative at first, nodding and grunting one-word answers to my questions. When finally he did speak, his few sentences ripped apart my smug, simplistic moralism.

Unlike his "buddy", he did not have the academic qualifications to dodge the draft by going on to university. Nor did he have the wherewithal to relocate. He was just a working-class boy from New York.

"What choice did I have?" he asked.

What was really getting to him was the moral judgement he felt he was subjected to.

"They call us baby killers," he said bitterly.

Yet he had only done what he had to do in order to survive.

Denny had been really clever, he told us — dodging the draft by paying for university tuition in France. But his money came from a well-paid summer vacation job "in a factory that makes the flame throwers we used in Vietnam".

This was said without rancour, a statement of fact about the unfairness of life for someone of his station.

We left Palavas the next day, when the weather had cleared. Danny said no more, bidding us farewell with the briefest of nods. And we never mentioned that conversation to Den and Bonnie, who saw us off as we paddled toward Sète. But over the following weeks and months and years, that conversation with Danny had a longer-lasting effect on me than almost anything else on the voyage.

CHAPTER 13

Being blasted by the Mistral

The Mediterranean port of Sète, near Agde, is the easternmost of these two French ports linking the Mediterranean Sea with the Atlantic Ocean via waterways across the length of France. The Canal du Midi runs from Sète to Toulouse. There it connects with the Canal de Garonne and the Garonne River, which flows into the Atlantic at the Gironde Estuary beyond Bordeaux.

Devised by a former tax collector turned canal visionary, Pierre-Paul Riquet, and his engineer partner, François Andréossy, the Canal du Midi took fifteen years to build and was a phenomenal feat of engineering. Riquet and Andréossy supervised thousands of miners, artisans and peasants, who dug by hand and used gunpowder for the first time to blast through rock to construct the canal. The waterway was fed with water funnelled in from streams and a reservoir they had also built, in mountains more than thirty kilometres away. In the process they built bridges, aqueducts, and a tunnel allowing the passage of the Canal du Midi through a hill.

The canal was completed almost exactly three hundred years before we ventured into the last kilometre or so to see what post might be awaiting us in Sète.

Sète itself was a welcoming sight: a number of yachts, a barge, fishing boats and other miscellaneous craft were moored alongside in the little harbour. Among them was a small wooden clinker-built craft with a cabin flying the Union Jack. Two young men were sitting in the stern.

"Can we moor next to you?" I asked.

"You're welcome," they chorused and helped us aboard as we made *Amandla* fast.

They were lads from Boston in Lincolnshire who had converted an old lifeboat into a waterborne mobile home, but after a rough crossing of the English Channel, had decided they'd had enough of the sea.

"Went out here once," one of them said of the water beyond the harbour.

It seems they had hit some rough weather, fled back to port and hadn't left again for months.

There was also a couple who had sailed from Australia and were waiting to cruise the Med in the summer. And then there was the older man who had bought an old Dutch barge, brought it down to Sète and was in the process of converting it into what he said, with great foresight, would be "the future for the canals"— a floating hotel.

We were very happy to find mail awaiting us in Sète and also delighted to discover that there was a public bathhouse. For a minimal charge, hot water in large enamel baths was available throughout the day and into the night. Men to the left, women to the right. And no rowdiness allowed. That meant no singing, with any breach of this regulation causing a raucous bellow from the bathhouse attendant. It was the greatest treat we had enjoyed since leaving England, particularly now that the weather was closing in.

The multi-national group moored alongside in Sète all slept aboard their vessels. We obviously could not manage that in the kayak, and we became somewhat envious of the larger, better-equipped craft. But we soon discovered a small, secluded stretch of beach down by the breakwater where we could pitch our tent. It was within easy walking distance of the colony by the quayside and the public baths. Our mode of transport was also decidedly cheaper than the bigger vessels.

The Lincolnshire lads promised to take us out in their boat when the weather cleared, to give us a feel for the waters beyond the outlet. Because of their bad Channel crossing, they wanted "really calm" seas before venturing out beyond the harbour.

However, local fishing boats did go out on most days. We watched them in the morning, hauling out nets of squirming eels they said were to be "sold to Italy for Christmas". Would the eels be jellied, we wondered, thinking only the English were eccentric enough to eat such things. We also tried our hand at fishing, from the shore and from the harbour walls — without success.

Although most of the vessels in Sète were tied up for the winter, we felt we couldn't stay on. We had, after all, turned down the offer of a Caribbean cruise from Aigues-Mortes because we were in a hurry to get to Gibraltar and do the crossing to Tangier.

Although we would also have to wait for the sea to calm down before venturing out, we had no intention of leaving from Sète. Our plan was to continue along the coastal waterway through the Étang de Thau, a lagoon that virtually links Sète with the other terminus of the Canal du Midi — Agde. It would be much more pleasant and would allow us to add this great waterway to our itinerary.

"Wait for the Mistral," the fishermen told us.

This wind that blows from the north would supposedly clear up bad weather. What they failed to mention was that the Mistral is often bitterly cold and can blow for days on end at speeds of one hundred kilometres an hour or more — as we were soon to find out.

After a couple of days there was a slight break in the weather and we said our goodbyes and pushed off, away from the public bathhouse and the hot baths, back up the harbour and into the lagoon. This stretch of salty water is listed as one of the largest lakes in France and forms part of the Canal du Midi. At the western end it links to the Hérault River and to the great circular lock with its separate gates leading in three different directions, each with different water levels.

This lock, completed in 1676, is another brilliant display of engineering by Riquet and Andréossy. While we waited vainly in the circular lock, hoping we would be allowed through without having to portage, I mentioned how fascinating it would be to see some of the inland areas of the famous Canal du Midi.

"Don't even think about it," said Barbara. "Anyway, we are probably

24/11/67 GREETINGS TO YOU BOTH FROM THE ... PAR AVION ... 0.25 RÉPUBLIQUE FRANÇAISE aix 0.60 ... DENT

The harbour walls at Agde, the terminus of the Canal du Midi

going to have to drag our way out of this."

She was right. There didn't seem to be any lock-keepers around and people we signalled to on the shore all seemed to indicate that we should portage. That meant lifting *Amandla* out of the lock onto the shore and wheeling our way down to the river and on by water to Agde. Eventually, and with some difficulty, we did just that, satisfied that we had covered the thirty-two kilometres from Sète in good time.

One of the oldest towns in France, dating back some 2,500 years, Agde, like Baix on the Rhône, had been washed over by the tides of history. The Phoenicians and Greeks had settled here and it had played an important role in the establishment of Roman Catholicism in France. But we couldn't tarry. Besides, there seemed nowhere in the town where we could stay. So, after having a minor problem with my camera fixed, we headed down the five kilometres to where the Hérault meets the sea.

Rounding the southern wall and its small lighthouse, we spotted something similar to Sète — a stretch of sandy beach. Only there was also a hotel and what appeared to be shuttered holiday homes set a little way back. We landed and were greeted by a man who turned out to be the caretaker of the hotel. Everything, he said, was closed for the winter. He directed us to a deserted campsite behind the dunes. It was cluttered with sand-clogged old German blockhouses and gun emplacements, minus the guns. Perfect, except that even the shops in the area seemed to close out of season.

Once again the weather threatened to close in as we hiked back into Agde to pick up supplies. At the post office we sent off a postcard that announced that, once the weather had cleared, we would "head like a rocket down the coast" to pick up mail at our next *poste restante* — Cerbère, right on the Spanish border. What we failed to mention was that the weather, even when "clear", was extremely cold. On some mornings in the campsite the flysheet of the tent was rigid, the condensation during the night having turned to ice.

In cold and even quite foul weather, we could manage on the canals. So, despite Barbara's initial reluctance, we considered paddling back through Agde into the Canal du Midi to link with the Canal de la Robine. This would take us further down the coast to Port-la-Nouvelle. The Canal de la Robine dates back to 1776 and was built to link the city of Narbonne with the sea along the route of the River Aude. But it meanders through the countryside for 108 kilometres and there were more than fifteen locks. Too much time, we decided. We would leave from the beach beyond Agde and just cut across the sweep of the Guld of Lion to Port-la-Nouvelle where the Canal de la Robine empties into the sea.

Eventually the weather cleared and so, again without consulting any fishermen who might know about the vagaries of climate, let alone checking on any weather forecast (had we known where to find one), we packed up our campsite one morning and pushed off into gentle breakers.

There was a slightly chilly, light breeze blowing and it was our first venture into the sea since our rather haphazard paddle along the English coast to Dover. But we soon settled into a steady rhythm, paddling about one kilometre offshore across the long sweep of the bay and making what we thought of as good time.

In the first of our hourly paddling breaks, we cut through a large wave and Barbara was drenched by spray.

"I hope salt water is good for the complexion," she said sarcastically as she wiped down her face.

At midday we paused for our inaugural lunch at sea: a couple of apples, biscuits and some nuts. We ate reclining on our lifejackets in the watery sun, gently rocked by the swells. It was still rather chilly, but held out the promise of my "Summer Holiday"-style expectations of the Mediterranean leg of the voyage.

There were no other craft to be seen and, as the afternoon lengthened, there was no harbour in sight. However, we had for some time noticed a long stretch of sandy beach and houses to the north. We assumed this was Narbonne Plage, so we swung *Amandla* round, estimating that we had covered about forty kilometres. As we neared the beach, we caught a wave that carried us right up onto the sand.

Our guess was correct; this was Narbonne Plage. The beach was perfect, gently sloping up to a short stone wall behind which was a road and a row of large holiday homes. All the shutters were closed. As in Agde, the "real town" must be beyond the beachfront, we thought.

Sheltered by the stone wall, Barbara set up the kitchen while I scoured the area for rocks to hold down the guy ropes and tent pegs in the beach sand. The wind had picked up quite strongly and was very cold. Must be the Mistral, we concluded, not having a clue what that meant.

We were soon to find out.

Barbara had bought bread and pâté in Agde and we ate this as an

5/4/1968 YES, FOLKS, STILL HERE AT
NARBONNE-PLAGE (1) ...

The wide beach at Narbonne that grows even wider when the Mistral blows

hors d'oeuvre[29] before her delicious Narbonne Plage curry.[30] The sky had cleared, and was sprinkled with bright stars. Once we had washed the dishes, the worsening wind chill forced us into the tent and our sleeping bags. What seemed like only a few hours later, but must have been in the early morning, we were woken by a noisy flapping on the side of the tent: in the howling wind the pegs holding the flysheet had pulled out of the sand, the rocks I had found not being heavy enough to hold them down.

I crawled out and managed somehow to grab hold of the flapping flysheet and, with a combination of rocks and tied-together guy ropes, stop it from flying away. By the time the sun was rising the wind had picked up even more. This was the Mistral, howling down the valleys of the Rhône and across the Camargue, battering our tent in a way I

---

29 starter
30 Barbara's recipe is on page 199.

had thought impossible. I found and carried rocks. And more rocks. Despite the slight shelter of the wall, and with every guy rope weighed down with rocks, the wind still seemed likely to rip the tent, rocks and all, off the ground.

We had pitched tents in drizzle and even quite heavy rain, sometimes with the wind blowing. But never in wind like this. Finally, though constantly buffeted, the tent stayed up in one position. We watched, appalled, as the sea retreated, pushed back by this incredible force of nature. The beach grew wider and wider still, with depressions of pooled water soon dried up by the wind.

As we peered dejectedly out of the tent, we began to feel like abandoned extras in a scene from some post-apocalyptic film. There were no people, no animals, no signs of life. Dried vegetation, like the favoured tumbleweed in scenes of ghost towns in Western movies, scooted silently across the deserted road and beach toward the retreating sea. Even the now clear, azure sky seemed ominous as the wind shrieked, with no let-up. No wonder all the houses were shuttered. But where was everybody?

Most of that day was spent securing and re-securing the tent or playing travel Scrabble inside to try to take our minds off the wind. I think we opened a can of beans and finished off the remaining curry for supper that night as we huddled in the tent.

"Don't worry," I assured Barbara, "it'll blow over."

But all that blew over was our shelter. Perhaps the wind subsided slightly during the night, but early the next morning we woke up tangled in the tent.

After extricating ourselves we checked that *Amandla*, low against the wall and secured by rope and rocks, was still intact. Then we weighted down the canvas tent, flysheet and all, with our sleeping bags inside, intending to pitch it again once the wind dropped. Only it didn't.

Meanwhile, we staggered around the holiday resort of Narbonne Plage in the gale, finding no signs of life. It was weird, quite frightening.

Finally, feeling miserable, we returned to the beach to look for heavier rocks to hold down the guy ropes, before again struggling to erect the tent. We probably didn't even eat that night, as the Mistral continued to howl around our now rock-bound shelter.

The next morning we decided that we had to find a living soul. So we staggered along the deserted streets, heads down and hats secured, often having to hold on to one another as we were hit by particularly strong gusts. We chose a different route from the previous day and, as we reached the corner of a street, there was evidence of human habitation at last: a small restaurant, and the door not shuttered. Through the glass there seemed to be people. Well, at least one person.

Arms linked, we stumbled across the road and opened the door. We were greeted by a look of utter amazement on the face of the man we had seen, and a gasp from a woman — presumably his wife — standing behind a counter. We must have looked a sight in our bright orange anoraks, with the hoods pulled up over our bush hats and tied down firmly to stop our headgear from flying away.

We introduced ourselves and tried to describe, in our unreliable French, how, having come from London in a kayak, we had ended up in Narbonne Plage.

"*C'est fou!*"[31] the husband said to his wife in a just-audible whisper. Given the Mistral, it obviously was.

It turned out that the *patron* of the restaurant and his wife were the only full-time residents in Narbonne Plage. They lived above the beachfront business that was "very busy" throughout the summer season. But in winter it was very seldom that anyone came by, except for occasional workmen repairing homes for the season or people who had lost their way.

We had not exactly lost our way, but we were famished. And, had we not found the restaurant, we'd have had to turn to our army surplus

---

31 "It's mad!"

emergency supplies. This was too good a chance to miss. Was the restaurant open for business? No, said the *patron*, but, with a glance at his wife, who nodded, he said it would be open for us.

They had — like most French restaurants — three set meals at varying prices. We went for the cheapest: a three-course lunch (including salad and a meat dish) that cost, from memory, 11 francs each. It was delicious. Along with a bottle of wine and freshly baked bread supplied by our hosts, we received a crash course on the wind, much of it highly mythologised.

The Mistral, the *patron* said, blew away all the dirt and muck and pollution, but it was known to drive animals and people mad. And it always blew for periods of either seven, eleven or fifteen days. In very bad Mistrals, some elderly people had been blown away, never to be seen again. Cars and trucks could be overturned and people had been frozen solid by the icy gusts while seeking protection in the open. Sometimes, he added, this ill wind would pause for a day or two after an extended blow and then start all over again. This one was clearly an eleven-day blow, he said.

Thanking our hosts, and enlightened by the myths of the Mistral, we stumbled our way back through harsh reality to our kayak and rock-bound tent. Suddenly a Caribbean cruise on *Shalimar*, away from the European winter and the Mistral, became very appealing. The problem was our mail was waiting for us in Cerbère, more than forty kilometres across the bay, and *Shalimar* was back in Aigues-Mortes. We decided to "sleep on it" and hope that some solution would present itself.

But in order to "sleep on it" we had first to erect the flattened tent. Neither of us is sure how we eventually managed it, but it did involve more rocks and the weight of *Amandla*. By then it seemed that one of the tales about the Mistral told to us by the restaurateur had to be true: it could drive people mad. Inside the tent seemed no better than outside and, as night fell, we couldn't use our "*bougie* power" for fear that the wind-buffeted tent would make contact with the candle and set us ablaze.

Eventually we did get to sleep and the tent stayed at least reasonably erect.

"We've got to get out of here and away for winter," said Barbara as we tried to re-fasten and tighten loose guy ropes the following morning.

I agreed. Marc, *Shalimar* and the Caribbean suddenly seemed a gift from the gods. We were back to emergency rations when, the next afternoon, a solution presented itself. It came in the form of a man from Narbonne, fifteen kilometres to the north, who had come down especially on a Wednesday to check on one of the holiday homes, fearful that the Mistral might have loosened tiles or shutters.

He was a caretaker, he explained. Many of the homes were owned by people as far away as Paris and they only came down in the summer months, mostly May through to July.

We politely enquired if they — or he — would mind if we stored our kayak in one of the garages?

"*Pas de problème*,"[32] he said.

He had some work to do the following day, so he would bring down the key to the garage almost exactly opposite our camp. And, since he usually came down to check on the houses every Sunday, we could expect to see him if we returned on a Sunday.

He was as good as his word. By midday, on Thursday, 30 November, *Amandla* was safely locked away in the garage. The Narbonne Plage caretaker also offered us a lift to the road leading to Perpignan and Cerbère, which we gladly accepted. We were ready to travel on land, having made backpacks out of roped-up groundsheets containing our various basic possessions. Mine with the tent tied on top. I also had my camera around my neck, and typewriter in hand.

Only minutes later, having wished one another bon voyage, Barbara and I were on the roadside, thumbs outstretched.

---

32 "Not a problem."

CHAPTER 14

Caribbean hopes & a hut in Aigues-Mortes

The Mistral was still gusting its way across the landscape, which was probably why so many cars and trucks flashed past without acknowledging us. Eventually we made it to Cerbère, where mail was waiting.

We sat in the post office and Barbara penned a hasty postcard to her parents, and I a quick note to mine. Then we sat looking at one another. It was obvious that we had reached the same conclusion. We would crew for Marc on *Shalimar*, sail to the West Indies and back, then pick up *Amandla*. In what we believed would be a calm Mediterranean summer we would head straight to Gibraltar and across to Morocco.

Once in Gibraltar or Morocco, I suggested, we might look again at fitting a sail, and maybe even an outrigger, to the kayak so that we could move faster along the North African coast. Barbara merely nodded. But I was sure after a two-way trans-Atlantic voyage and a return to a balmy Mediterranean summer, she would be convinced.

"You mean barmy, as in crazy, right?" she said.

Even this failed to undermine my enthusiasm. I assumed she was joking.

That was how, by mid-December, we were back in Aigues-Mortes, being warmly greeted by Bill and Muriel Kerr on *Wanderbird*.

This time we also got to know some of the local residents. And a few of them expressed concern about us living in a tent beside the walls of the city.

"*Mon dieu,*[33] you cannot even stand up inside that *très petite*

---

33 "My God"

Once a fishing village: Cerbère on the Franco/Spanish border

maison,"[34] someone said.

They were probably also worried about our toilet arrangements, knowing that we had to trek into town to use the public ablutions. We were certainly not going to inform them about the screw-top "piddle jar" kept for cases of emergency and carried in a bag to be emptied in the public toilets.

Their concern was misplaced; we were perfectly happy where we were. But then one of the families decided to help us. They owned a *"petite maison"* out in the asparagus fields. This little home had its own running water, they said, and we would no longer have to crawl into bed. Presumably, they had no objection to some natural fertilising of the fields.

How could we say no? It was impossible. So, after expressing our

---

34 "tiny abode"

thanks, we trekked out to the *petite maison* a short distance from Aigues-Mortes. It was a solid wooden shed and it did have a tap with what seemed to be potable water. There were also a number of large sheets of heavy plastic, probably used for roofing, and some crates that we assumed were for the asparagus crop. Here we had the makings of a bath, and with smaller crates and some loose planks, a dining table and a kitchen with chairs. With plenty of water and the means to heat it, I duly lined a large crate with plastic sheeting and we were in business.

It was a relaxing, if shallow, warm bath in the open air, with the added attraction of what seemed like an almost never-ending succession of magnificent sunsets. As the brilliant orange-hued sky faded to rust and night fell, we had a good lamb-chop meal under the stars.[35]

"It's good to be able to *stand* and cook for a change," said Barbara.

While we tidied up and retreated indoors, we concluded that our French friends were right: their *petite maison* was an improvement.

It all seemed very snug as we blew out the candle. But we had no sooner settled into our sleeping bags than there were sounds of frantic scuttling, followed by the patter of little feet: the place was overrun with mice. It was our first — and last — night sleeping in what we then disdainfully referred to as "the shed". In the morning we set up the tent outside and made sure that it was zipped up tight at night.

Every day we made our way into the ancient city and to the harbour. Marc, the top of his head visible in an open skylight of the forward compartment of *Shalimar* — his atelier[36] — would be painting.

"For an exhibition," he would explain. "I need forty or fifty."

But after several days of constant painting, he would retire to relax in the stern of *Shalimar* with a bottle or two of vodka. It was only later that we discovered that while he was sleeping off his

---

35 The recipe for Barbara's "Sunset lamb cutlets Provençale" is given on page 201.
36 studio

hangover, his wife would take several new paintings and drive away. She apparently sold them and, by the time he came to, he was again behind for the promised exhibition.

It was a game that had apparently been played for many months — a clever, and profitable, delaying tactic.

We later heard that she had confided in one of the stallholders in the market that she was terrified of the sea. But of all this we were blissfully unaware. It took some time to realise what might be going on, although the Kerrs would nod and smile knowingly when there was any mention of *Shalimar*'s touring prospects.

"Just a few more weeks and we are away," was Marc's mantra.

And I suppose we believed it because we so wanted to sail off to the Caribbean and put winter behind us.

In the meantime, we explored Aigues-Mortes and played Lotto (Bingo) in one or other of the restaurants where it only cost a few cents a card and where a cup of coffee or glass of wine was inexpensive. We never laid claim to any of the Lotto prizes, even when we thought we qualified. Not only because we were unsure of having heard the numbers correctly, but because these often comprised live trussed chickens or pheasants and, once, a rabbit. Sometimes we would spend an evening playing Scrabble with the Kerrs while becoming better acquainted with the local wines.

My conversational French also improved, courtesy largely of Gauloises cigarettes. I discovered that it seemed perfectly acceptable in these parts to conduct a conversation with a Gauloises dangling from the corner of your mouth. This meant I could fudge the fact that I hadn't a clue about the difference between "*la*", "*le*", and "*les*" in a sentence. Genders, singulars and plurals were beyond me. And my nasal pronunciation (try speaking with a cigarette dangling from the corner of your mouth), along with a tendency to slur my vowels, worked. "*Vin*" was a clipped "vang", which was exactly how the locals seemed to pronounce it, often along with the Spanish "*si*", instead of "*oui*".

Every week, on Sundays, there was a market in the ancient square, with brightly coloured umbrellas and a wonderful variety of produce at good prices. The atmosphere, despite the chill in the air, was warm and festive. On 17 December we enthused in a postcard home about the decorative Christmas lights being switched on in the square.

At that stage we had not yet begun to worry about *Shalimar* perhaps not leaving. Besides, we had a lot of catching up to do, since neither of us had ever crewed on a yacht before. Fortunately Bill Kerr had a good library of books covering every aspect of seacraft. We were not going to repeat the haphazard, Michelin road map approach to the Caribbean voyage.

We read up about basic maintenance, navigation, self-steering and the various (many) do's and don'ts from those who had carried out Atlantic crossings. All the while we assumed, without ever checking, that Marc was an accomplished skipper. It bolstered our confidence to discover that he was right about the time to sail from Europe across the Atlantic, although we thought he should get going very soon.

We were relieved to find out that we would be avoiding what sounded like the rather dangerous Bay of Biscay by heading out through the Strait of Gibraltar. Then — and Marc concurred in the few brief chats we had with him — we would swing left and head south, borne on the warm breezes from the Sahara, "until the butter melts". This would be followed by a right turn to catch the winds to carry us westward and so on down to the Caribbean. It would be about three weeks of very hard work with probably little sleep. But we were young, fit and dead keen.

At the same time, we heard and read a lot about the region: about the Camargue and its wild horses (which we never saw), the bullfights of the south of France (which we never saw either) and the ancient and chequered history of the region. Perhaps unsurprisingly, there was little mention of World War II, because, we supposed, the Languedoc had been the centre of the collaborationist Vichy regime. Awkward matters of the past had apparently triggered a generalised amnesia in the cause of national reconciliation.

We avoided such issues, but mainly because our very basic, grammatically appalling French was not good enough to carry an argument. Which is also why we never broached the question of the local obsession with "*la chasse*" — hunting. Every so often, especially at weekends, sitting outside our shed in the early mornings, we would hear the putt-putting of a motorised bicycle as a hunter came into view, shotgun or rifle slung across his back, often with a dog in a basket in front of the handlebars. In the distance we would also hear the bangs of guns being fired.

We heard that, in the Languedoc, the hunters sallied forth to seek out the *sanglier*[37] that apparently populated many of the small copses of woodland that dot the French countryside. From August to February, the season of *la chasse,* hunters would set out, sometimes several times a week, armed with rifles or shotguns, adequate sustenance for the compulsory long lunch, including wine, and a flask of "something stronger". We never saw a wild boar, nor heard of one being shot, but we did sometimes see a hunter returning with what looked like a string of dead sparrows hanging from the handlebars of the motorised bicycle.

The dogs, too, were something to behold. They came in all shapes and sizes, but were mostly quite small, a far cry from English Pointers and Setters.

"They're not real gun dogs," said Barbara, as we watched a group of hunters and their dogs head off across the fields.

Didn't mean a thing to me, but Barbara's father had bred Pointers. And, from an early age, she had accompanied her father on field trials where dogs would find prey, point and then fetch whatever was shot.

"Perhaps they're just there to scare up whatever they shoot," she said.

We never found out.

---

37 wild boar

By then we had become part of the local scene; nobody stared at, or commented on, our bush hats any longer. And we would exchange greetings with stallholders in the market and nods and smiles of recognition in restaurants or bars on Lotto evenings. However, our French was not up to scratch, and we were still very much outsiders looking in.

We also continued to avoid, whenever possible, having to share another local obsession: a liking for pastis, that anise-flavoured apéritif that is sometimes referred to as the "milk of Provence". But it was sometimes impossible to decline when offered one by someone who considered it a nectar of sorts. And we would reciprocate, although never daring to state a preference.

This because, as we quite soon discovered, there is not just one pastis. Nor is there just Ricard and Pernod, labels we had earlier spotted. There are other varieties, each of them bearing their own myths and provenance. Our French was certainly not adequate for the intense debates that erupted from time to time about the merits of one pastis above another. And certainly not up to making an argument against all pastis.

There were also some older men in the bars who, almost misty-eyed, would mention "absinthe", an apéritif that had pre-dated pastis and was reputedly strong enough to "kill a bull". It had been banned decades earlier because of its alleged hallucinogenic qualities, but nods and winks implied that it was still available "around and about".

We neither saw nor tasted absinthe, though it might have helped us cope better with the chilly, and often damp, weather. But we were buoyed up when, a few days before Christmas, Marc finally made an announcement: "We sail in the new year."

The Kerrs, who invited us to share Christmas dinner aboard *Wanderbird*, had, until then, been quite circumspect about Marc and his grand Caribbean plans. Yet, with hindsight, there were several hints that all might not be as it seemed. The Kerrs obviously hadn't wanted to dampen our enthusiasm.

There was no mention of the couple from *Shalimar* coming over for the Christmas dinner, for reasons that became obvious in the course of the meal. It was then that we realised that Bill and Muriel had always seemed rather doubtful about when — even whether — *Shalimar* would set sail.

The English couple had shopped in the local market and Muriel produced a roasted shoulder of lamb with roast potatoes and an assortment of vegetables, something she could manage easily in the yacht's well-appointed galley. After our limited repertoire of one-pot meals, we savoured — and later remembered — every delicious mouthful.

As promised, and using our recently acquired anniversary day lesson, we also sought out a couple of bottles of Crémant de Limoux, the sparkling wine of the Languedoc region. To this we added several delicacies from the local patisserie for dessert.

It was a grand Christmas, and Bill took the opportunity to warn us of the likelihood that *Shalimar* would not be going anywhere. He pointed out that although she was a fine vessel, there was no evidence that Marc had any experience as a skipper. Anyway, said Bill, when *Wanderbird* had arrived months earlier, *Shalimar* was already berthed at Aigues-Mortes and Marc was even then promising to leave at any moment.

We began to worry, because by then we had accepted — very reluctantly in my case — that it was impossible to contemplate canoeing at sea until at least the spring. Pottering about in other canals was a quickly discarded alternative, as was staying put in Aigues-Mortes — we simply could not afford it. Besides, we still found it difficult to believe that Marc had involved us in an elaborate ruse to stay put while pretending always to be on the verge of setting sail. But the new year came and went and we finally had to accept that *Shalimar* would not be leaving.

We hadn't really wasted our time, but we were running out of our £50 export allowances. Perhaps, if we could get to Gibraltar, a British territory, we might be able to have some of our savings transferred from London to top up our funds for the rest of the trip. *Amandla* was tucked away safely in a garage in Narbonne Plage. In any event the weather in Gibraltar was bound to be warmer and — if costs were not too high — we could base ourselves there while we sorted out our finances. If we wanted to live more cheaply, we could always go across to Morocco.

So, after fond farewells to Bill and Muriel and rather less fond farewells to Marc and his wife, we packed up our tent in the asparagus fields and set off with our makeshift rucksacks on our backs. After a slight detour to Cerbère to pick up mail and arrange for a forwarding *poste restante* address, we put our thumbs up and made for the Spanish border, aiming for the Rock of Gibraltar.

CHAPTER 15

Jock of Gibraltar & the horror of Monte Cassino

I n Spain hitch-hiking was much more difficult than in France. There were not as many private cars and truck drivers were wary of taking more than one passenger at a time for fear of attracting the attention of the local police — the Guardia Civil.

We did get one long ride in a battered flatbed truck. Two elderly men had just delivered a load of fish that had obviously been covered with wet hessian bags to keep them fresh. However, by the time they picked us up, the bags in the back of the truck were stiff, smelling and speckled with fish scales. I was hidden under those bags, ensuring

The east of Gibraltar with the great water catchment area

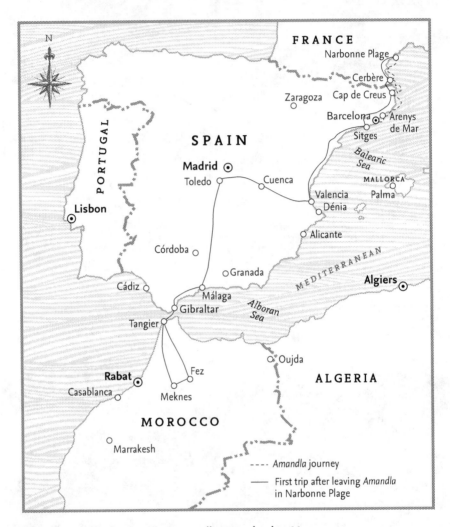

Leaving *Amandla* for the winter; travelling overland to Morocco

that I developed an abiding horror of the smell of fish. It was a long and, for me, singularly unpleasant ride.

I had a brief conversation with the drivers (as much as mime and very limited Spanish would permit) before I was relegated to the back with the fish scales. They hinted that they were not in favour of the Franco government and relished the thought of breaking the law. Later, sharing the cab, Barbara was regaled with tales that clearly indicated that they were not only involved in the Civil War — "bang, bang, '36" — but were almost certainly anarchists.

We were grateful for the ride, but after I had cleaned myself off as much I could in a railway station restroom, we decided it was best to carry on to the Spanish border town of La Línea by third-class rail. At least I had taken my hat off and tucked it under my anorak before being covered by the sacks. It did not smell.

There was no problem getting onto the Rock from La Línea, apart from the slightly unnerving revelation that we had to walk across the Gibraltar airport runway to reach the city.

"You must stop if a plane is coming," the immigration official warned.

Once across the runway we entered a cultural pastiche. Post boxes and shop signage in the city seemed at once English and yet not quite. Nor was the atmosphere really Spanish, in a tiny territory that had voted overwhelmingly in 1967 to remain a British possession.

There were also notable peculiarities, such as the fact that water in the cheaper rented rooms and apartments was only available in large earthenware containers, much like Roman amphoras. As we very soon discovered, water was a critical issue on the Rock. There was none. In order to survive, the various garrisons and residents on this tiny vestige of imperial power had to rely on rain. On the eastern side of Gibraltar was an enormous concrete catchment area.

Most accommodation was fairly pricey and we soon discovered that the only alternative in Gibraltar, short of illegally camping out in one of the many caves on the Rock, was "Jock's TocH Hostel". This retreat, behind the South Bastion of the city's protective walls, was probably the first of what were later to become the ubiquitous "backpackers" around the world.

The name puzzled us. It was known colloquially as "Jock's", but also as "TocH". We later learned that the original TocH was a Christian rest house set up in 1915 by the army chaplain Reverend

Philip ("Tubby") Clayton in the town of Poperinge in Belgium, a few miles from the trenches at Ypres. It was initially named Talbot House, but soon became known by the soldiers as TH, and then, in radio signaller's code, as TocH. After the war, it became a Christian charity, based in England.

We turned up to be welcomed to "TocH" by a stocky, elderly Scottish man with a shock of white hair — Captain William Boyd ("Jock") Brown. We later discovered that this venerable organisation had, by then, refused to have anything to do with "Jock's". Or with Jock Brown for that matter.

So far as TocH was concerned, the hostel that had once been its outpost on the Rock was entirely Jock Brown's affair. He had made it so after refusing in 1959 to close it down and return to England to run a "sea-going boys' hostel" in Southampton.

Accommodation on the Rock was not plentiful and the premises originally occupied by the TocH Hostel, with dormitories, a kitchen, games room and library, far exceeded the needs of the radically reduced, post-war British garrison. But the rest and recreation facilities provided by TocH for British and Allied service personnel were in full use, mostly by what Jock Brown referred to as "shoestring travellers".

Within months of the end of World War II, Jock had noticed "lads turning up in Gib" who had been there before. They were rootless. They had often gone through hell and couldn't settle down, he said. They had little but their demob pay and an urge to travel.

In those days before widespread recognition of post-traumatic stress, many were left to their own devices, unable to adjust to life out of uniform and unwilling or unable to stay within it.

On Gibraltar, Jock bent the TocH Hostel rules. Most of his early travellers no longer had any connection with the military — and never wanted to again. So Gibraltar's TocH became a backpackers' refuge, unofficially subsidised by the military and by TocH.

Eventually, the eviction order came. But, for the authorities, the timing was bad: Britain's Queen Mother was scheduled to visit Gibraltar and the TocH Hostel was on the route she was to be driven around the tiny British territory. So, with members from the remaining garrison, sailors in town and local supporters, Jock Brown, on the night before the scheduled royal cavalcade, carted all the beds and bedding out onto the pavement to illustrate the reality of eviction.

According to several local dignitaries, the authorities panicked. If Jock would just remove the offending objects from the Queen Mother's route, he could have the South Bastion as a new home for his hostel. The deal was done and Jock moved to the South Bastion, taking with him beds, bedding and other equipment.

The South Bastion was a far cry from the original facilities, although it had been tarted up a little by the time we arrived in January 1968. There was the original powder store with its metre-thick stone walls, which was Jock's home, and two large lean-to buildings down either side of the bastion walls, one containing double rooms and the other a double-storey dormitory block, with a TV/games room on the lower floor. Near the entrance was a half-collapsed tunnel leading to what were allegedly the dungeons in which shackled convicts were held on their way to penal colonies in Australia and elsewhere.

On a small piece of ground alongside the hostel was an old British Post Office van. Its once bright red livery was a pale pink, but it had new tyres. It had been driven from London to Gibraltar by a couple who ran out of money and the desire to travel. They left it at the hostel, telling Jock he could have it for the price of two tickets home. So Jock inherited the van and put it up on blocks to save the tyres, and there it had stood for several years.

On the roadway outside the South Bastion, there were also several parking bays, one of which was occupied by a small British Bedford van with a glass-fibre pop-top roof: a perfect example of an early self-contained motor caravan. This was the home of Kenneth Edward Steel Muggleton Kenmar, a dapper, intense Englishman, always keen to engage in conversation. He was the designer and builder of the — by then well-known — Kencat catamaran, who also happened to be one of the original prisoners of war featured in the largely fictionalised box office hit film *The Great Escape*.

"I was the one with the limp who couldn't join the escape because I had broken my leg when we were shot down," he explained.

In the weeks we spent at the hostel in Gibraltar, it became obvious that he qualified as one of Jock's "lads" who could never settle after the experience of war. He thought the kayak venture was marvellous and talked about it so widely that we ended up being interviewed by Gibraltar TV.

Jock, on the other hand, never mentioned our venture and also spoke very little about himself. It was only years later that I managed to piece together the life of this Scots coal miner who went to war as a Gordon Highlander in 1914. He saw action both at Ypres and the Somme, was wounded twice and rose through the ranks. He emerged from that carnage a dedicated pacifist and a member of TocH.

What intrigued us, especially given the source of our kayak challenge, was Jock's obvious affinity for Canadians, although he maintained contact with hundreds of former travellers. When we arrived, in January 1968, he was still in the midst of completing his responses to Christmas cards received. He had 553 to go, from former soldiers, sailors, airmen and a host of later "shoestring travellers".

Then, one unforgettable evening, when I was chatting with him in his one-time powder-store lair, I discovered why he felt a particular kinship with Canadians. A keen photographer, Jock had been sorting through some of his wartime prints when I called in. He invited me to sit down and, his memories perhaps jogged by the images, told me about his experiences at the Battle of Monte Cassino between May and June 1944.

When World War II erupted, Jock volunteered to provide sustenance — "tea, buns, soup and sympathy" — to the troops as a member of the

Navy, Army and Air Force Institutes (NAAFI). He established a mobile canteen that followed the troops throughout the Allied invasion of Italy.

In those fearful, blood-soaked months between January and May 1944, Jock Brown's NAAFI mobile canteen moved up the road toward Rome behind the Allied troops that were stalled at the entrance to the Liri and Rapido valleys. Dominating this area was a mountain topped by a 1,500-year-old abbey. Allied forces called in air strikes that dropped 1,400 tons of high explosives, destroying the abbey, but not seriously damaging the German forces dug in lower down. The ruins, in fact, made for better cover.

Polish, Moroccan, French and British troops fought and died on those slopes defended by well-armed and supplied German paratroopers. But Jock and his canteen and camera were with the Canadians. And it was Canadian armour that was brought in to add power to the Allied push.

"They always send in the infantry first," Jock said bitterly, obviously remembering an earlier war. "But there were lads out there lying wounded when they sent in the tanks, right over them."

He had the photographs to prove it. They were gruesome. He showed them to me that once, but refused to bring them out again for anyone.

By then Barbara and I had already spent two weeks at "Jock's" at a time when anything more than a day or two in one place, let alone a week, was considered unusual. We were also fortunate to have booked in at the same time that Gladys Street was in residence.

Gladys was an Australian, a widow of many years who, then in her seventies, made a bi-annual pilgrimage to Europe from her home in the Blue Mountains outside Sydney. She always based herself at "Jock's on Gibraltar". She was something of a walking encyclopaedia of the cheapest places to stay on the Spanish and Portuguese coasts.

"Great place, that one," she would say about a particular recommendation. "Only avoid the third floor. Bloody noisy — it's a brothel."

She effectively managed Jock's while she was in residence, checking that bedding was cleaned and properly fumigated. Travellers coming in from Tangier's doss houses could bring with them both lice and bed bugs, something we also later discovered to our horror. She kept trying to persuade Jock that all those booking into the hostel should pay in advance. This was a policy Jock refused to follow, insisting that "we should rely on the honesty of everyone".

In a tone of great affection, Gladys would mutter, "Silly old fool."

Dubbed "Lady Gladys of Street", to her obvious delight, she surreptitiously collected money in advance from every traveller and, when the backpackers left, turned it over to Jock. This would invariably result in a brief lecture about how this was evidence that "when it comes down to it, most people are honest". Gladys merely shrugged.

While she was in residence, everything operated like clockwork. Jock put this down to a belief that most people, if left to their own devices, would behave in responsible ways. He was, to the end, a committed idealist whose dreams, in many ways, crumbled about him.

In 1968 it was obvious to us that there was a different type of "shoestring traveller" moving through Gibraltar. These were no longer the post-war lads Jock Brown still idealised: alienated former conscripts from a global conflict, disillusioned that the world they thought they were fighting for had not materialised. Now there was a range of youth, mostly from fairly affluent backgrounds, who were cynical about the world at large, experimenting with drugs and taking a break from a real world they would return to. They usually saw themselves as part of the "turn on, tune in and drop out" flower-power generation.

But there were also American draft dodgers, assorted radicals, adventurers, misfits and romantics, an eclectic collection of young North American and European humanity. Jock was aware that they did not accord with his vision of the "shoestring traveller", but this he blamed on bad influences beyond Gibraltar, and especially in

Tangier. They were still, fundamentally, the same "lads and lassies" he had always known.

There were several to whom he used to write who were in prison in Canada and the United States. After falling foul of the law, they contacted him and he always seemed to reply. Invariably, he admitted, "the lads" had been convicted of drug offences. He blamed Tangier. This was why he wanted to open a hostel in the Moroccan city.

He suggested that Barbara and I might like to undertake such a venture at some stage. He would let us take the old pink Post Office van to Morocco as temporary accommodation.

"No way," said Barbara when we were out of earshot. "Not Tangier. But why don't we just stay on Gibraltar?"

I did not share her enthusiasm for the Rock, but agreed that we could consider it — once we had paddled there in *Amandla*. I think I saw this as a way to inspire her to continue with our journey. My general disorganisation, coupled with the sojourn on Gib, had apparently dampened her always-less-than-enthusiastic approach to the kayak venture. But I imagined that, after we had paddled into Gibraltar, she might be inspired to continue to Africa and Dar es Salaam.

In the meantime, we became something of a fixture at the South Bastion, much like Kenneth Edward Steel Muggleton Kenmar and Lady Gladys of Street. With corrugated iron, planks and poles, delivered to the hostel by a well-wisher, we even built another double room against the back wall of the bastion and were surprised to see it still standing when we returned to Gibraltar on a visit in 2008.

By 1968, when we met him, Jock's health was obviously failing. He was often in pain and would grumpily retire to his powder-store home, refusing ever to go to a doctor. Whenever he felt "poorly" he would don his kilt, determined that if and when he "went out" it would be "as a Scotsman". Probably the most memorable character we have ever met, he died in Gibraltar in 1969 and is buried in the local cemetery.

CHAPTER 16

Important lessons in Morocco

After turning down Jock's offer to start a kindred hostel in Tangier, we decided to spend the rest of the winter in Morocco. It was warmer and considerably cheaper. We had, in any event, replenished our finances in the same way wealthy, yacht-owning Britons did: transfer money to Gib and change it into any currency, even into sterling traveller's cheques. The £50 annual export allowance was a farce if you were rich enough to sail a yacht to Gibraltar or if you happened to find your way to the Rock.

The bank in London, probably aware of this, sent a questionnaire that seemed to be aimed at determining whether we were now resident in the British possession, Gibraltar. Since we were living there at the time, we were, of course, resident. We duly notified the bank of this — and the money was transferred.

On the eventful trip to Tangier that had led to Kent Warmington's kayak challenge, we had travelled to Algeciras, across the bay from Gibraltar, and taken the ferry across the strait. The Rock loomed large on the port side as we sailed out, bound for the tiny Spanish colonial toehold of Ceuta in Morocco. From there we had taken a bus to Tangier.

This time we took the ferry from Gibraltar directly to Tangier.

During the five weeks in Morocco, most of it spent in Tangier, we also hitch-hiked around a number of areas, learned some Maghreb Arabic, and became properly acquainted for the first time with couscous and harissa. Perhaps more importantly, we became familiar with some of the local customs, especially regarding hospitality.

Aware of the relative poverty of the people we met and got to know we felt that, when invited to share a meal, we should somehow compensate. We twice made the blunder of shaming our hosts by

Fez: home to the oldest university, with living history everywhere

patronisingly stepping in to help pay for their hospitality. It was an object lesson about insensitivity and the unthinking arrogance of so many in the wealthier, developed world.

In one case, we were given an excellent example of one-pot cooking by a man called Mahmoud, who sold primus stove prickers — devices for lighting and cleaning paraffin stoves. We were staying in the same cheap medina hotel in Tangier and, perhaps because I had greeted him with a few of my newly acquired half a dozen words of Maghreb Arabic, he invited us to dinner in his room. He had only one large suitcase in which he carried all his possessions, including pots and a primus stove.

It was a wonderful demonstration of organised cookery that Barbara marvelled at, to his evident delight. He told us that he travelled through the desert areas, mainly by camel, and every six months would come to "the city" for a couple of weeks to experience a different life. And it was an honour to invite us, visitors to his land, to a meal.

It was a superb meal: a spicy stew with couscous, followed by sweet mint tea.[38] In the process of chatting in our limited French, a few words of Arabic and much mime, I noticed that the shirt collar of what was probably his best shirt was slightly frayed. I had one good shirt that I hadn't worn on the trip, so I excused myself, went to our room and came back to proudly present him with the gift of the shirt.

The salesman was gracious when he accepted my gift, but even then I sensed something was wrong. As he cleared away the plates, he announced that he had something special for us on the following night, something we would marvel at. And he was insistent. The "something marvellous" was a movie, screened onto a rather wobbly screen in a medina hall, with the audience seated on wooden benches. It was "Joseph and his coat of many colours". In French, with no subtitles. And he took us several times.

I think I realised then what I had done, because we had noticed how this tradition of hospitality, linked to the Islamic alms-giving of *Zakat al-mal* (tax on wealth), was abused by a number of the young travellers. They would go, barefoot, begging in the streets while waiting for the next substantial allowance from "home", usually sent via American Express.

Some claimed that they were on a journey of self-discovery; that they were trying to experience what it was like to be among the poorest of the poor. But this was an obscenity in which a centuries-old tradition of mutual help became a self-indulgent emotional playground for rich kids, most of whom seemed to spend their allowances on copious quantities of hashish. The two centres for this behaviour were Tangier and Marrakesh. After weeks in Tangier, this was one of the reasons we headed for the ancient city of Fez and on, briefly, to Meknes.

---

38 Barbara has described her versions of these, on pages 206 and 209.

Fortune smiled on us. On the road out of Tangier, we were given a lift by an officer in the Moroccan army — Hadji Bouz-Bouz. He not only ensured that we had a good, reasonably priced pension in which to stay in Fez, but took us on a night-time tour that included the parts of the ancient walls of the Fes el Bali, usually closed to tourists. This is the oldest part of Fez, founded in about 800 CE and declared a World Heritage Site in 1981.

Aigues-Mortes had the ancient walls, but here were all the ancient crafts, practised as they had been for ten and more centuries. And by people who looked as if they belonged to an age long past. This was living history. Unsurprisingly, as Hadji Bouz-Bouz proudly informed us, Fez also housed the oldest continuously functioning university in the world.

To end off the tour, Hadji Bouz-Bouz took us to a café in the former *Quartier Français*[39] where we ordered coffee and pastries. There he also met up with some of his friends and, while they were chatting at another table, I forgot my lesson with Mahmoud and called over the waiter and paid the bill. I don't think either Barbara or I have ever eaten so many pastries or drunk so many cups of coffee over a few hours as we did into the early hours of the following morning. And there was a degree of frostiness as Hadji Bouz-Bouz wished us farewell when he dropped us off at the pension he had arranged.

I hoped I had learned a lesson from this, but in the years that followed and in the various, sometimes complex, cultural milieux in which we became immersed, I often wondered: how does one give and take graciously and with equanimity? Perhaps it is best to talk openly about cultural expectations and *mores* and clear the air before any gaffes ensue.

As we left Fez, after a two-day stay, the weather was balmy, and I relished the familiar sensation of warmth. It reminded me of home.

---

39 The French Quarter

"The hat," I incautiously joked to Barbara, "is happy to be back in Africa."

To which she replied, with a smile, but in a tone that indicated that she was serious, "Then why don't we just keep going?"

This was mutinous talk and I was having none of it. I insisted that we had a commitment; we had, at the very least, to get back to Tangier before there could be any discussion about changing course. She shrugged and we headed for Meknes, another ancient city, smaller than Fez, but in many ways just as grand. This fourteenth-century city was expanded hugely in the seventeenth century, using largely European slave labour.

It was difficult to find a place to stay in Meknes, so after some all-too-brief sightseeing, we headed back to Tangier, where we knew our way around and had a convenient, clean and cheap place to stay. Because we had also got to know some of the shopkeepers and stallholders in the market, we were also no longer bothered by the youthful touts.

But Tangier was seedy and there were worrying aspects such as the level of obviously impoverished child labour. Besides, it was almost April and, perhaps lulled by the more clement Moroccan weather, we decided to head back to Narbonne Plage to rescue *Amandla* and resume our paddling.

This time, with our augmented funds, we could take advantage of the fact that Gib was a duty-free port. Cameras, the new, portable reel-to-reel tape recorders and other electronic devices were much cheaper here than anywhere else in Europe or North Africa. So, on returning from our sojourn in Morocco, we purchased one of the first portable aluminium-cased Ricoh tape recorders. It would go with us from Gibraltar, via Spain and France, to Narbonne Plage.

The Spanish and Moroccan authorities were always on the lookout for these products, on which duty could be charged. The way to avoid paying such taxes was to ensure that any products bought new on Gibraltar looked older and used, as if they had been bought in other countries. Various techniques had been developed over the years — passed down from mouth to mouth — that made it almost impossible for the authorities to determine whether a product was new and bought in Gib. Needless to say, soon after the reel-to-reel tape recorder came into our possession, we made sure that its cover was suitably "aged" and contained a tape referring to events months earlier in France.

By the time we got back to the Rock, Gladys Street had left and Ken, of the British Bedford van with the fibreglass pop-top roof, proposed that he become our "land base". He would follow us along the coast and rendezvous whenever we landed. We politely turned him down. A man who could take the better part of an hour to play one tile in a Scrabble game was not, we thought, the best person to operate such a base. Besides, we had never needed anything like that and it threatened to cramp our style, such as it was.

We were feeling ready for the next phase of our adventure, although Barbara had developed what appeared to be eczema around her neck. It was very itchy. I was not worried, as she had mentioned how, as a child, she had been allergic to all variety of things, from cat hair to pollen. I, on the other hand, prided myself on being allergic to nothing.

At least the weather seemed to be improving and our travels around Morocco had given our legs much-needed exercise and our shoulders and arms some rest. I confidently told Jock and Ken that they could expect us to paddle into the harbour at Gibraltar "by June". We would raise our hats to salute them as we passed the South Bastion.

CHAPTER 17

Braving the sea and bells in the buff

The weather was pleasant enough as we travelled up through Spain by train before hitch-hiking to Narbonne Plage. But when we got to the notorious *plage*,[40] the wind was blowing. Not quite the Mistral, but gusty and somewhat cold.

We set up camp in about the same spot where we had, after a fashion, weathered the Mistral. The caretaker was true to his word. Three days later, on his Sunday rounds, he turned up and opened the garage for us. We trundled *Amandla* out of the garage and back onto the beach. The caretaker left and Narbonne Plage was again deserted. It was surreal, as if we had gone to sleep in the Mistral, had nightmares, followed by great dreams of travelling, only to wake up exactly where we had been stranded.

The weather had not yet cleared and the sea was still much too rough for us to even attempt a launch. But at least we could cook next to the windbreak provided by the wall and the tent did not seem in danger of blowing down again. Barbara's itch hadn't cleared up either, but she was trying to be stoical about it.

"Out on the sea, your allergy will disappear as fast as it came," I reassured her.

Two days later, the weather lifted.

"Let's go for it," I said.

Barbara looked up warily at the few scudding clouds.

"Hope the good weather lasts," she said.

We packed up camp and ensured — as best we could — that all was well stowed, and I put our travelling clock and compass into a pocket of my anorak. Then we guided the prow of *Amandla* into the gently

---

40 beach

lapping water. We both wore the elasticised waterproof skirts that would fit over the cockpit rims when we were seated and hopefully keep most of the water out of the kayak, even in quite heavy weather.

With Barbara in her cockpit I pushed off, slipped into the rear cockpit and started paddling.

I was on a high. We were at last really on our way. The canals, the rivers, the waterways were mere practice; here was the real thing. We would zip along the coast, popping in here and there at seaside villages and fishing ports. There would be no more locks, no more waiting on barges; we would simply scoot along at our own pace.

Once we were into deeper water and free of breaking waves, I called a halt as I reached inside the skirt for the clock and compass in my anorak pocket. I did this single-handedly. The other hand was holding the paddle. I found the compass and put it on the canopy. Then I went back for the clock. As I brought it out, a slightly larger wave hit and the compass slid off into the sea.

In my frantic attempt to grab the compass, the clock followed suit. All of this behind Barbara's back.

"Oh, hell!" I yelled.

With a jolt, Barbara looked over her shoulder, her face registering her "Rhône River look"— sheer terror.

"The clock's gone overboard," I gabbled.

Barbara looked relieved. "Never mind, we never used it much, anyway," she said.

The knowledge of a compass in our possession seemed to provide Barbara with a sense of security, so at that stage I thought it wisest not to mention that the compass had also gone to the bottom. Anyway, I thought we would have no need of one around the Mediterranean. We had no intention of paddling very far offshore and, even in that fogbound shambles in England, the compass had been of limited value.

Although the sea was choppy, with a rather brisk and chilly breeze blowing, it was not unpleasant paddling. As we got into our stride, Barbara acknowledged that it was good to be on the water again.

However, it was extremely slow going: the pace was often no more than five kilometres an hour. After a while, with heaving water the only scenery, it became quite boring. We decided that, if the wind picked up further, we would head to Port-la-Nouvelle a little over twenty kilometres away. If the weather improved, we would go on to Port-Vendres, fifty kilometres or so further down. Perhaps we would even paddle as far as Cerbère.

After our lunch-break snack, the wind strengthened and clouds began to roll in. The sea became very choppy. So we pulled in closer to the coast and headed for Port-la-Nouvelle. This seemed to be a large commercial port, so we would have to land *Amandla* outside the harbour entrance.

We scoured the beach and found a protected spot to come ashore and pitch our tent. Fortunately it was just a short walk to town to stock up on supplies; we had used up all we had while waiting in Narbonne Plage, where there were no shops or markets. At least it wasn't raining and our campsite was protected enough to be quite comfortable.

I started setting up the tent as Barbara prepared a Port-la-Nouvelle dinner, to be accompanied by a celebratory bottle of the local *vin rouge*.

"The sea did nothing for this allergy," said Barbara, scratching her neck. "I must have been bitten by something."

I immediately pronounced this impossible, since I did not have the same problem.

"If something was biting you, it would have bitten me too," I said.

Before we turned in to bed the wind seemed to drop, although the sea seemed no calmer.

"Summer is coming," I announced.

Barbara was not convinced.

"Don't be daft. It's still April," she said.

That night in Port-la-Nouvelle we slept well and woke the next day feeling refreshed. Getting dressed, I decided to put on a black polo-neck shirt I hadn't worn since Morocco. To check that the neck was properly rolled, I turned it back. Barbara maintains that I shrieked. I maintain that I gasped. Inside the roll-neck, all the seams were white — lice.

I was appalled. Disgusted.

"I've been complaining for weeks about bites to my neck," said Barbara. "And you dismissed it as eczema."

I frantically examined my hat, turning it inside out before I tore out of the tent, pulling on some clothes, and raced into Port-la-Nouvelle. There I bought cans of what I was assured were the most potent insecticides available. Then back to the tent, where I proceeded to spray every seam of the tent and much else besides, giving special attention to my hat and polo-neck shirt.

"Don't be so bloody neurotic," Barbara said, watching me with something like amused detachment.

"We're getting out of here," I announced. "We're going to Portbou."

Portbou was just across the border in Spain. Small pension hotels in such places often prided themselves on the hot water they provided and they were a lot cheaper than anything in France. So we bundled up every item of clothing and material we had — anything with a seam that could hide lice. Then we lashed down the kayak and, with our clothing secured in our makeshift groundsheet backpacks, sprayed inside and out, and with typewriter and tape recorder in hand, we set off for the railway station. On the way, despite an exasperated look from Barbara, I stopped to buy two more cans of insecticide.

It was Friday, 12 April 1968, when we booked in to a pension in Portbou. Only after being assured by the manager that the water available was not only hot, it was "*muy calor*"[41]. In fact, he maintained,

---

41 "very hot"

it was quite dangerously so. "*Muy bien*,[42] just what we want," I assured him.

We were shown up to a large room with a shower cubicle, toilet and double bed with impeccable white linen bedclothes. I tested the water from the shower. It was not just hot; it was close to boiling. Perfect. We opened up our packs on the tiled floor by the shower cubicle and stripped off what we were wearing, and I proceeded to spray each and every item again, ignoring Barbara's insistence that I was going overboard.

I also insisted that we throw away a couple of white items, since we could not spot lice on them. These were sprayed, bundled up and thrown into the rubbish bin. Then I spread items of clothing and my canvas shoes on the shower-cubicle floor and turned the scalding hot water onto each of them, a process repeated several times.

"We're probably being poisoned by the insecticide," Barbara said as she watched my frantic efforts.

When that process was complete, I insisted that we pile all the clothing into the cubicle and jump on it as we each took a shower. Only then did we go near the towels provided by the management.

Barbara seemed to find the whole process extremely amusing.

"Overkill, I'd say. But I suppose we're cleaner now than we'll ever be. Totally hygienic. Pity we have no dry clothes."

I had at least brought the long length of nylon cord that I tended to travel with and this we strung up as a makeshift washing line. Soon the room was festooned with wet clothes. I admitted that I had acted somewhat irrationally. But then, I explained, we had been travelling with those horrible little creatures ever since Barbara had first complained of an itchy neck. My skin crawled at the thought of them crawling unnoticed all over us.

In my mad rush to get to Portbou I had left behind our cooking

---

42 "Very good"

equipment and basic supplies, so by the Saturday afternoon we were faced with the prospect of either going hungry or venturing out in freshly washed clothes.

The latter won the day. In wet jeans and T-shirt and wearing damp canvas shoes, I left the pension and bought bread, cheese, sausage and a bottle of local wine for a late lunch.

During my excursion I passed a bar where a group of men were standing outside, talking loudly, apparently about a forthcoming midnight mass. It was only then that it dawned on me that it was Easter. Considering we were in a very religious country, the men seemed to be rather cynical about the whole business, waving dismissively toward the church higher up the street. They good-humouredly pointed to one of their number, urging him toward the church and laughing amid comments about going "*con tu esposa*".[43] That much Spanish I understood. They were apparently joking with him about being hen-pecked.

That evening I suggested that, even though our clothes were still far from dry, we should venture out to a bar and "catch up on some local colour". So, sitting in damp shirts, jeans and shoes, we sipped beer in a bar whose patrons were exclusively men, among them some I had seen earlier that day. Judging by their gestures and facial expressions, they seemed to be adopting the same dismissive approach to the coming mass. But they all seemed rather better dressed. For all their apparent cynicism, they would be heading up the hill come midnight.

We didn't wait to see if our assessment was correct. We were back in our room shortly before midnight, with tape recorder in hand. We hung up our clothes again and, standing on the small balcony overlooking the street, we were able to record for our parents the bells of the church up the hill summoning the Portbou faithful to mass.

We said nothing on the tape about lice, accusations of neurosis,

---

43 "with your wife"

insecticide, hot water or that the bells were recorded as we stood stark naked on a first-floor balcony. There are some things that are better left unsaid.

By the Monday our clothes had dried. We repacked and decided to take a look at the coast that we intended to paddle along soon. For the equivalent of five cents each, we travelled fourteen kilometres by train to the second protected inlet port along the aptly named Costa Brava (Wild Coast). With the cloud-capped Pyrenees Mountains to one side, we sat on a rocky promontory some six metres above a wild sea, the waves sending spray up high enough to reach us. The sea was too rough to consider paddling in it, but the little harbour was completely calm, protected by a natural breakwater.

"This is a truly magnificent sight," said Barbara. "Even more beautiful than anything I've seen in South Africa."

I agreed.

"Not being in a canoe at sea right now is good," she added.

I was quite oblivious to any implied criticism about the venture. Apart from the sea conditions, this was what I had imagined the bulk of the voyage to be: gorgeous scenery and idyllic little fishing harbours.[44] So, after admiring the natural beauty and the neat white cottages with blue doors and red shutters, we headed back to Port-la-Nouvelle to resume our journey.

---

44 In 1968 the garish, multi-storeyed developments that followed the growing invasion of especially British and German tourists had not yet reached this far up the coast.

CHAPTER 18

The magnificent Costa Brava & early warnings

We arrived back in Port-la-Nouvelle in high spirits, although the Easter weather had churned up the sea somewhat. It might be a day or two, we thought, before conditions calmed down and we could set out for the magnificent Costa Brava.

As we reached the beach and spotted *Amandla*, it was obvious that the sea had come up and moved the kayak well away from its mooring. Then, as we got closer, we saw that the cover had been opened. We raced over to discover that our tent and gas stove, both of which had been readily accessible on the cockpit seats, were missing.

"If you hadn't panicked and got all neurotic, we could have found a safe place to store our things," Barbara said. "Or we could have taken the tent and the stove with us."

I had to admit that when I spotted the lice I was in no mood to listen to any advice.

"*Mea culpa*," I said.

It was obvious that this was going to knock a hole in our finances. But Barbara had another suggestion.

"Let's just pack it in," she said. "Give it up now."

"Don't be silly," I replied. "You're just upset because the tent and stove were stolen."

With that, I walked into Port-la-Nouvelle and bought another gas stove and a new, yellow tent. It was two metres long and about one and a half metres high, with a built-in blue groundsheet and flysheet — almost a replica of our earlier accommodation.

Back at the beach, when the new tent was up, it looked slightly bigger than the previous "two-man" tents we had carried.

"I can just about stand up in it," Barbara said.

I was still restricted to sitting down or moving on my knees.

We forgot about the cost and Barbara made a consolation meal: a sumptuous stew of chorizo sausage, haricot beans and tomatoes, which she called "Cheat Canoe Cassoulet".[45] But we had lost the better part of a week, what with the sea conditions and the lice. And our position at Port-la-Nouvelle was not ideal for launching. The beach had been devoured by the waves, leaving a considerable drop to the water.

"We'll portage," I said. "Go by train to Port-Vendres and set off from there for Spain."

Barbara looked relieved as *Amandla* went back onto her wheels and we trundled off to the station for the short trip to Port-Vendres.

Had we been able to launch at Port-la-Nouvelle, it would have taken us the best part of a day to get to Port-Vendres. By train we were there in less than an hour and a half.

Port-Vendres in those days could be accurately described as "a charming fishing port". Like so many natural harbours along the French coast, it dated back many centuries and had at one stage been settled and developed by the Romans. Its importance from a military perspective was evidenced by the fortifications built as far back as the seventeenth and eighteenth centuries and as recently as World War II. A focal point in the town was the thirty-metre-high marble obelisk commissioned in 1780 to celebrate the American War of Independence, the end of serfdom in France and, I thought contradictorily, free trade and the strength of the French navy.

We liked Port-Vendres and would have considered staying on if the weather had not changed for the better. Shortly after 6 a.m. on 19 April, we set off from the harbour into a gently swelling sea, turned right and headed for Portbou.

Ahead of us, to the north-west, lay the Pyrenees: great, stark mountains that seemed to rise up out of the plain, dividing France from Spain. Reaching heights of more than 3,000 metres (10,000

---

45 This recipe is on page 203.

feet), they extend for nearly 500 kilometres from the north down to the Mediterranean, where a cliff, like a cut from some giant's knife, seems to have removed the rest of the range.

There was a broad, single yellow line painted high on the cliff face and extending downward for several metres to where the mountains abruptly ended, sheering off into the sea.

"Pass that and we're in Spain," I announced.

We paddled strongly until we reached the bay that in those days housed all that was Portbou.

Turning right, we made our way toward the beach, where fishing boats were drawn up. Higher up the mountain, by the train station and immigration post, we could see uniformed figures coming down toward the beach: Guardia Civil, Sten guns and rifles in hand. They got to us just as we hauled *Amandla* up onto the pebbles and sand. We tried to explain as best we could where we were headed, but they looked puzzled. They shrugged and asked us to accompany them up to the immigration office to have our dual passport stamped.

There were many more questions and much shaking of heads as we explained, largely by mime, how we had come through France and along the coast. It was all very friendly, but, judging by the looks we got, they considered us crazy. They also gestured that they thought our hats peculiar, which seemed a bit rich coming from people who wore shiny pillbox hats with a flat panel on the back.

One of the officers also asked, with a look of concern, about Cap de Creus. I answered enthusiastically that we were headed that way. His eyes widened and he shook his head ominously. We didn't pay much attention. We were relieved that we were now legally in Spain, and hopefully would not encounter further problems.

In the end the police officers wished us *"buen viaje"*[46] and two Guardia escorted us back down to the beach. They watched with

---

46 "bon voyage"

evident amusement as we pushed off from the shore.

It was getting on for midday, so we decided to pull into the first convenient bay along this fabulous coast for lunch. We soon spotted a small cove with a sandy beach and paddled in. There were a few people about, but nobody paid us much attention as we found somewhere to sit down and picnic.

We had packed up and were preparing to launch, with Barbara already in her cockpit, when we were greeted by a family who said they were from Manchester.

"You're the ones that are paddling to Africa," they chorused.

We admitted that we were.

They seemed extremely impressed that we had got as far as we had, which made us feel a little better about the delays.

"But we've got a very long way to go," I said, as I started sliding *Amandla* back into the water.

"I insist you have this," the father said, and he pressed several hundred Spanish pesetas into my hand and wished us good luck.

We tried to persuade him to take it back. But he retreated and waved us off. We waved in return, paddled out of the bay and turned south around the Punta del Frare, still hugging the coast, with its jagged rocks and little inlets, coves and caves. It was a warm day, on a calm sea, and we were moving at a fair pace.

We had by that stage managed to get hold of a fairly good tourist map of the shoreline, but it hadn't conveyed just how spectacular it was.

"We should stay around here for the next few weeks," Barbara suggested.

I hoped she meant it only half-seriously. But while I wanted to get on to Gibraltar, I agreed that this was too good to miss. So we explored the intriguing jumble of rocky crumbs from the Pyrenees, taking the channel between the mainland and the islands of Illa Grossa and Illa Petita[47] and across the bay to the Punta del Boro.

---

47 "Big Island" and "Small Island" in the local Catalan language

We both felt that was the best day of the entire voyage so far.

There were a number of other small rocky outcrops, coves and islands as we powered our way through several bays and past the Punta de la Figuera and the port at Llançà, to El Port de la Selva at the eastern base of Cap de Creus. Apart from a one-hour delay in Portbou and a brief stop for what turned out to be a lucrative early lunch, we had been paddling for ten hours when we finally ran *Amandla* onto the beach near the yacht harbour at El Port de la Selva. We planned to camp there. Given the ins and outs along the coast, we had probably covered more than fifty kilometres. We certainly felt it in our shoulders, but we were extremely proud of ourselves.

Then everything was put into perspective as we heard those Mancunian voices greeting us again as we walked up to the road leading to the harbour. They had driven down to El Port de la Selva along the coast road and were about to get into their car to return to their holiday apartment.

"It was just a quick spin, thirty minutes up the road," said the father.

They wished us good luck again, refused to take back the money and drove off.

According to our map, there didn't seem to be any habitation anywhere on Cap de Creus. It didn't help to find out that there are points on the cape glorified by names such as Cova de l'Infern, meaning Cove of Hell. Given the reaction of the Guardia captain in Portbou, I thought we should make a few enquiries.

There were a number of yachts in the little harbour and fishing boats pulled up on the harbour beach. This seemed a good place to do some research. When we asked people on the yachts, we were regaled with a series of hair-raising tales. The currents around Cap de Creus! The rocks! The dangerous winds that had brought many a vessel to grief! One French yachtsman was particularly insistent: the cape was "*très dangereux*"[48] and it would be unwise to attempt

---

48 "very dangerous"

to round it until well into the summer.

However, the fishermen were far more sanguine, and a couple of them spoke some English. They agreed that the cape had a notorious reputation, but with our kayak, they thought we should have no problem, especially in the right weather. Yachts, sailing too close to the rugged coastline and facing variable winds, had sometimes come to grief. We should stay close to the shore and, if anything bad blew up, we should be able to make landfall, although they didn't think that would be necessary.

They also pointed out that, with our shallow draft, we should be able to get in really close to the garden wall at Port Lligat on the opposite coast, where Salvador Dalí lived. The great surrealist artist, they said, hated anyone intruding on what he considered his bay. He would come to the wall, shouting and waving a stick. We should look out for him.

Nobody mentioned fog and the thought of that particular phenomenon never crossed our minds.

But we were extremely nervous when we went to bed that night.

"If the weather's right, we take it easy and tomorrow go around to Cadaqués on the other side of the cape," I said. Then, in a weak attempt to lighten the mood, I added, "We may even see Salvador Dalí."

It didn't work. Barbara merely nodded agreement and said, "Only if it's really calm."

As we were dozing off in our sleeping bags we were suddenly woken by the sound of the tent zip opening. The muzzle of what turned out to be a .303 rifle appeared, along with the barked command: "*Pasaportes!*"[49]

There were two Guardia in their olive green uniforms and their strange pillbox hats. They ordered us out of the tent. I scratched about at the back of the tent to find the passport, put my hat on, and emerged, with Barbara following. While one of the Guardia kept his

49 "Passports!"

134

rifle pointed at us, the other, obviously in charge, slung his weapon over his shoulder, produced a torch, and leafed through the passport I handed him.

"What a cheek," Barbara muttered loudly, and the Guardia with the torch glared at her as he handed me back the passport.

I waited anxiously, hoping Barbara wouldn't decide to add a few more choice words. Although she never claimed to be a sailor, she could certainly swear like one.

Fortunately she didn't.

He said something in Spanish, but all I could make out was "*A donde?*"[50]

"Cadaqués," I said.

"We leave tomorrow, I mean *mañana*,"[51] Barbara added.

"*Bien*,"[52] said the one in charge and, with a dismissive wave, he turned and walked off down the beach, his companion following him.

We crawled back into the tent.

"You can take your hat off now," said Barbara.

It was some time before we finally got to sleep. We were wondering whether armed police patrolled every beach every night, and if this amounted to institutional paranoia.

In London I had met members of the International Brigades: international volunteers who had fought on the Republican side against the Nationalist forces in the Spanish Civil War. They maintained that such paranoia was part of the means of control in Francoist Spain. We decided that, just in case, we would keep the passport handy at all times.

We woke fairly early, despite our interrupted night, and had a leisurely breakfast. All the while we anxiously scanned both sea and

---

50 "Where to?"
51 "tomorrow"
52 "Good"

sky for signs of trouble. But, apart from a few clouds, the sky was a deep, clear blue and the water reflected this as it lapped gently onto the beach.

"We've got to go," I announced as I started packing the kayak.

"All right," said Barbara in a less than enthusiastic tone.

CHAPTER 19

In fog without a compass

It was Saturday, 20 April, that we faced the prospect of paddling around Cap de Creus. I don't think either of us had ever been so nervous before or has been since. It wasn't just the warnings and tales of the yachting fraternity, the caution of the fishers or the attitude of the Guardia captain in Portbou; by then I think we had both had enough experience to know just how inexperienced we were. But we were committed to continuing and there was nothing for it but to take the plunge.

It was at least 10 a.m. before we finally set off, paddling slowly but steadily out along the jagged coastline. Apart from the occasional slap of a wave against rocks and the sound of our paddles, it was silent — eerily so, at least in our imaginations. With its small bays and numerous little inlets into which rivulets ran, the coastline around the cape was nowhere near as wild as we had expected or been led to believe. In any other circumstances I think we would have marvelled at the sights, but instead we ploughed on nervously.

One of the fishers had told us that, at the point of the cape, there was an island — Illa s'Encalladora. We should take the channel between it and the cape and we would be on our way to Port Lligat and Salvador Dalí. We eventually reached the island and the channel, and made what was, in effect, a wide U-turn, heading down the western side of Cap de Creus and into a slight south wind from which we had, until then, been protected. It was a classic anti-climax. The water had become a little choppy, but nothing to worry about. We had conquered the dreaded cape.

"We're not there yet," said Barbara in an unexpectedly upbeat tone as we clung close to the shore.

Our proximity to the shore was just as well because, had we been a hundred metres or more out on the water, we might have missed the narrow entrance to the small natural harbour that is Port Lligat. We were still tense as we nosed into the cove and paddled close to the wall that we assumed was the property of Salvador Dali. But there was no sign of the great surrealist, so we swung out and continued paddling along the cape.

We knew we had been on the water for barely two hours, because as we glided into the beautiful bay that houses Cadaqués, the bell rang for the midday — Angelus — call to prayer, confirmed by the clock on the tower of the town's seventeenth-century church. We had made it. But we felt less elated than relieved, and the tension told — we were both exhausted. After a brief foray into the town, we decided to camp for the night and paddled across to a small, pebble-strewn beach with a series of terraces leading up to a house.

On the first terrace were signs in Spanish and English warning that the land was private. But the farmer who came down to greet us was friendly, welcomed us warmly and, in a mixture of French and Spanish, insisted we camp on his land. As we were pitching the tent, he returned with a large bottle of what he assured us was the best spring water anywhere. We thanked him for his generosity.

"What about staying over for a day or two?" Barbara suggested.

"It's tempting," I said. "But we're committed to getting to Gibraltar by June. Closer to that time and closer to the Rock, we can think of taking a break."

Hesitantly, Barbara agreed.

That night we had our expected visit from the Guardia.

It was quite a wrench to leave our terrace camp, pack up and push off from the beach. At least the weather remained unchanged: blue skies and a warm sun. The sea was clear and undulated gently as we headed out, away from Cadaqués.

Once again we stuck close to the shoreline, but only in order to appreciate the coves, beaches and hillsides. We took our time as we paddled into the Bay of Roses to where we could see the town of Roses with its lighthouse a few kilometres further into the bay.

Noticing a beach reminiscent of the beaches at Clifton on South Africa's Cape Peninsula, we paddled over and pulled *Amandla* up onto the sand. It would be a perfect place to camp. Because it would take a long time to follow the contour of the bay, I suggested that the following day we should instead paddle twenty-five kilometres or so straight across the bay to the western point at L'Estartit and then camp lower down the coast.

Barbara seemed slightly dubious, so I offered a compromise: we could camp at L'Estartit the following night and only go on if we "really felt like it".

"All right," she said.

That evening I made a fire on the beach with scavenged driftwood and Barbara prepared pasta and a tangy sauce while we waited for the inevitable arrival of the Guardia. We had just finished our meal when they turned up.

We greeted them and handed over our passport, which they examined closely and handed back to us. We asked for permission to camp on the beach and they nodded their consent. When they had left and we had put out the fire and cleaned up, we crept under an upturned fishing boat, our home for the night, and unrolled our sleeping bags on the soft sand.

When we headed out the next morning, the sky was still clear. However, once we got out of the bay, we found that the sea had come up somewhat during the night, with sizeable swells and some "white caps". This meant that Barbara was frequently struck by salty spray.

"There goes your complexion," I joked as we crested one swell.

She turned around and stuck out her tongue.

As we moved further from the shore I became aware of what seemed to be a bank of low cloud to the south. We were making reasonable progress, but the conditions were quite demanding as the cloud moved closer.

"Mist," I announced as we lost sight of the land ahead of us.

I promptly reassured Barbara that, since we could still see the sun, we had no problem.

But soon there was no sun. White-out. And the sea seemed to have become rougher. We didn't have a clue where we were heading.

"Get out the compass!" Barbara yelled.

Now, there are times when one regrets not having been totally honest. This was one of them. It was certainly not the most auspicious time to inform my partner and crew that I had lost the compass overboard. But there was no way of avoiding it.

On hearing my sorry tale, I recall her uttering a particularly vulgar expletive, something which to this day she denies.

Be that as it may, I decided that I should be responsible, so, in the calmest voice I could muster, I said, "Put on your lifejacket and put the passport and the money into your bra."

It was the wrong thing to say. Barbara simply turned around hurriedly, donned her lifejacket and then, in sheer terror, froze. I kept paddling, but I had to keep the prow or the stern into the waves. Had I not done so, the kayak could have gone broadside to a wave and capsized.

I also did a quick calculation that I didn't mention to Barbara. We had aboard five litres of water that could, at a pinch, last us for a couple of weeks. Food was less important. Even if we got caught in a storm and blown well away from land, we could survive. Still, the thought terrified me. It was a variation of the Inuit story that had started this venture.

"Don't worry, we're heading in to the shore," I told Barbara as I turned the kayak to run with the waves.

"How the hell do you know?" she shouted back.

I didn't, so I said nothing.

I didn't paddle hard, mainly letting the waves carry *Amandla* forward. If they were taking us to land that would be great, but if we were heading out to sea, there was no point in getting still further away from Spain.

At last the waves seemed to be breaking, which, I assumed, meant shallower water. And then there were the raucous squawks of seagulls. Closer in, the fog lessened and we could make out an expanse of beach. I steered *Amandla* towards it and we ran up onto the sand. Barbara leapt out, paddle in hand and stood, her back to me, as I pulled the kayak higher up. I was beaming, not only with relief, but also with perhaps misguided pride that I had somehow "got it right" and landed us safely.

When Barbara turned around, it was obvious that she did not share such feelings. And when I suggested that we get back into the kayak and paddle along within sight of the shore, she replied tersely, "No way. We walk."

The sand was too soft for the wheels, so I ended up wading in the shallows, towing *Amandla* whenever a wave broke on the shore. After an hour or so, Barbara agreed that this was ridiculous, so we pulled the kayak up and found a place to camp.

When the Guardia came that night we discovered that we had landed to the west of the famous Roman ruins of Empúries on the way to L'Escala. We must have paddled about five kilometres out into the bay before the fog struck and we would then have been perhaps eight kilometres or so out to sea from where we eventually landed, some twenty kilometres short of L'Estartit.

In the morning it was another clear day and the sea seemed quite calm. Barbara took her place in the front cockpit, but only after reminding me that I had promised no more short cuts. She insisted that the attempt to cut across the bay amounted to a short cut. From now on we would stick close to shore, no more than 500 metres or so, and, at the first sign of trouble, we would head for land.

And so we passed L'Estartit, a full day late.

There was no sign of mist, let alone fog, and the sea was as calm as we had ever seen it when we rounded the point and followed the coast, never straying too far from shore, even when there were bays to cross. It was warm and we got into a steady rhythm, stopping every hour for a break. Into the afternoon, probably somewhere east of Llafranc, we spotted the only other craft on the water: a rowing boat with a fisherman hauling in one of his lines. He landed a good-sized fish as we paddled up to greet him and ask about how best to navigate the coast.

He spoke a little English — more than our few words of Spanish — and we ended up spending a good hour or more talking while he checked the lines, his rowing boat and our kayak rocking gently, side by side, on the slight swells. He had several lines out and pulled in another fish while we chatted. On the bottom of his boat he already had a goodly number.

"*Grillados*," he explained about the fish — meaning that they were ideal for grilling. "A good catch," he said.

He was ready to head back home and wondered where we might be going. We explained that we camped on beaches and that the Guardia always came to check, because they were on every beach.

He laughed. "No, not every beach," he assured us. "It is a few that even the Guardia they do not know about it. *Venid! Venid!*[53] Follow me," he said with a wink and a knowing nod.

With the fisherman rowing ahead, we paddled slowly toward rugged, scrub-clad cliffs and a small inlet leading to a pebble-strewn beach with some straggly pine trees above the waterline. He had been using it secretly for many years.

We pulled up our boats and the fisherman indicated a level area where we could camp. He pointed to fallen pine cones and dried

---

53 "Come! Come!"

142

branches that would make a good fire. Then he bagged his catch and took out two quite large fish and handed them to us.

"To enjoy — *grillados*."

As he made his way to a steep and overgrown pathway up the cliff, he assured us again that tonight there would be no Guardia.

He was right. There was no-one and nothing to disturb us as we grilled the fish over an open pine fire under the stars, listening to the gentle hiss of the pebbles as the waves pushed them to and fro.

"This is what it should be like," said Barbara in a tone she had never used before about being at sea.

CHAPTER 20

Rough water & mutiny

As the sun rose the next morning we pushed off from the secret inlet. The sky was slightly overcast and there was a brisk breeze, but the sea was relatively calm. Soon we were paddling quickly down the coast.

As we paused for one of our breaks, I admitted, at Barbara's prompting, that this sort of paddling was very boring. It was hard work and we were avoiding all the interesting inlets inshore. The scenery was mostly water.

I didn't want to slow the pace, but since we were making very good time I agreed to swing into the coast, where we saw — and were duly horrified by — the multi-storey developments right on the beach at Tossa de Mar, followed by similar scenes at Lloret de Mar. The Costa was being destroyed.

"That's progress," Barbara remarked cynically, and we decided we would not stop.

However, as we passed that heavily built-up section of the Costa Brava, we realised that we were running short of fresh water. So we pulled into the beach at the next town — Blanes. While I looked for a place to fill up our water bottles, Barbara quickly dashed off a postcard to her parents. Then it was back to *Amandla* and launching into a sea that was becoming decidedly choppy, with a steady wind blowing.

As we were coming out of the shallow bay, the wind picked up further and we tended to be broadside to waves that were becoming larger. They were also starting to break even 500 metres from the shore; there was a danger of broaching,[54] as we had experienced in the Bay of Roses.

---

54 This is a nautical term meaning that there is a danger of capsizing.

Tossa de Mar in 1968 — start of tourism's desecration of the "wild coast"

We moved in closer to the shore and decided to make for what looked like a small, secluded stretch of beach beyond the town of Calella. It was quite a steep beach — more a small sand dune — right beside the pillars that carried a coastal road. We thought it perfect since it was extremely unlikely that many people would venture under what were effectively culverts under the road. We could walk through them to get to the town.

On closer inspection the beach, or dune, on which we landed seemed to have three levels, or terraces. We hauled *Amandla* up onto the first terrace and pitched our tent at the very top. The painter of the kayak was fastened to a large rocky outcrop almost under the roadway.

By evening it was obvious that there was quite a storm brewing, so we turned in early. When we woke the next morning the wind had dropped, but the sea was raging in and waves were crashing into the dune on which we were camped. The first terrace had been all but eaten away and *Amandla* was dangling over the edge, held only by the painter tied to the rock.

We rushed out and managed to drag the kayak up to the top of the dune beside our tent. There we stayed for the next two days, with occasional ventures into town, as the sea steadily eroded our dune. On the second night, the enormous waves seemed to be calming down and we celebrated with a chorizo and rice soup, using the last of our sausage supply. In the morning the sea had settled enough for us to be able to get away — once we had managed to get the kayak down a considerable drop to what had again become a stretch of beach.

However, the sea was still not entirely calm, and Barbara was concerned. I pointed out that, if another storm broke, we might not have the protection of the dune; it had probably been built up by wave action against the rocky outcrop to which we had tied *Amandla*.

She reluctantly agreed to our departure and we somehow managed to launch without getting completely wet.

"No more of this," I promised Barbara. "It's only a couple of hours paddle to Arenys de Mar."

I had decided that we would call in at this small port as it was almost certain to house yachts as well as fishing boats — and that meant hot showers. There was also bound to be a decent campsite nearby. We would treat ourselves and get some professional advice on the weather before setting off for Sitges in a long, one-day paddle.

The wind picked up as we headed out and Barbara complained about being constantly drenched by spray. After little more than an hour we noticed several small catamarans setting off from a beach and bouncing across the waves before turning around and sliding back onto the sand. Barbara pointed out that it would be perfect to land there, with the sailing boats. But I was sure we could make it to the entrance of the port of Arenys de Mar, no more than a couple of kilometres or so ahead of us, so I suggested we keep going. At that stage the wind had picked up and paddling had become difficult, but we persisted, leaving the catamarans well behind us.

I saw this as a particular challenge as I steered into larger swells, with spray splashing over us as we smacked into them. Barbara had by that stage stopped paddling and was holding her paddle up to avoid contact with the waves or with my paddle. The entrance to the port was right ahead as I battled to keep the kayak going forward. It was very heavy going, but at that stage I had only one focus — the Arenys de Mar harbour entrance.

We weren't making much headway when Barbara turned around and shouted, "That's it! Get ashore!"

It suddenly dawned on me that it was ridiculous to aim for the harbour. There was nothing much to gain from it. We could land on any part of the beach along the bay and walk to the harbour to consult people on the fishing boats and yachts — and enjoy hot showers. So I turned the stern into the waves and started to surf toward the shore. With a hundred kilograms of boat and gear and our combined weight, there was no way of turning *Amandla* out of the waves without possibly capsizing. I could only steer at an angle to the left or right.

I don't know who saw them first, but I think both of us yelled out simultaneously: "Rocks!"

We were heading for a rocky outcrop that extended to the left, toward the harbour. I steered to the right, straightened the kayak and caught a wave toward the beach. But, as at Calella, the waves had eaten away at the beach and created a small wall of sand beside the rocks. As we coasted in, I yelled to Barbara to throw her paddle ashore, jump out and grab the painter. The words were no sooner out of my mouth than the prow of the kayak ploughed into the wall of sand.

Barbara threw her paddle ashore, leapt out and scrambled up the sandbank. But she didn't take the painter. She stood there, atop the small sandbank, dripping water; her hat, anorak and face were soaked. I was also out in double-quick time to grab the stern of the kayak and the painter so that the next wave would not fill *Amandla* with water or even wash the boat away. At the same time I yelled to Barbara to catch the painter and help pull the kayak ashore. But she continued to stand there, her lips trembling and her fists clenched as the next wave drenched me. I managed to hold on to the kayak and yelled again to Barbara to get hold of the painter as I threw the rope to her.

It landed at her feet. But, instead of picking it up, she suddenly hunched her shoulders, glowered at me and shouted, "Eff you!" Then she turned and stormed off, just as another wave hit.

Fortunately, further along on the rocks there were three men fishing. They saw my predicament and rushed over, one of them grabbing the painter, and the four of us managed to get a slightly water-logged *Amandla* safely onto the dry sand. I thanked the men.

"*De nada,*"[55] they said, and went back to their fishing. I walked over to where Barbara was now sitting, dripping into the sand, and tried to console her.

She was inconsolable. She shrugged off my arm as I sat beside her.

"I'm wet. Everything's always wet. We can't go on," she said angrily.

I admitted that I should have listened to her when she suggested beaching where we had seen the catamarans going ashore. But I suggested that she should give me credit for my tenacity in almost making it to the harbour.

"We could have made it if you hadn't wanted to head for the shore. And I'd say I did a sterling job missing those rocks," I added.

All of this did not go down well. In the end I also had to admit that what I had seen as admirable tenacity could more accurately be described as "dangerous pig-headedness".

She pointed out that it wasn't just this one incident. The fog in the Bay of Roses and my admission that I'd lost the compass had been the last straw.

---

55 "You're welcome."

"I lost confidence in you," she said. "What you did was completely irresponsible."

I tried to lighten the mood by remarking that "the old hat" had seen us right and we had landed on a beach not too far from where we had intended going. In extremely colourful language Barbara told me what I could do with my hat. Then she pointed out that I didn't have a clue where we were heading in the fog; that all waves do not necessarily take one to the nearest shore; and that it was irresponsible to travel out to sea without a compass.

I had to concede that she had more than a point. Desperately looking around in the hope of changing the subject, I noticed that we were right beside a campsite. I suggested we set up camp and try to find some dry clothes. We obviously had a lot to talk about.

"Too damn right we have," Barbara snapped back.

With *Amandla* pulled well up onto the beach and the tent pitched, we changed into what Barbara referred to as "half dry" clothes and I rigged up a line to dry everything that had got wet during the landing. But wet clothes were the least of our problems: Barbara seemed insistent that she would not go on. And my jokes about mutiny did nothing to calm the situation.

I toyed briefly with the idea of suggesting that I go on in the kayak while Barbara carried on overland. But how? Walk or get a bicycle? On her own? It was clearly impossible; either both of us went back to sea or we both stayed on land. In any event, who would carry our dual passport? I am still grateful that I didn't make that "separate, but together" suggestion at the time.

I don't think we ate that evening. We probably got through our usual supply of fruit, nuts or whatever else was readily edible. But we talked.

Barbara acknowledged that she would travel with me on land in any conditions. She had done so before. And she would do so again. But the sea, she said, was a different matter.

"Bushcraft is one thing," she said. "seacraft entirely another. And hoping to gain the necessary experience while actually undertaking the voyage is, frankly, insane."

I disputed the insanity, but did admit that I had — or, rather, had had — a rather over-optimistic approach to the entire venture.

Even so, I argued that we had effectively given our word, in terms of the challenge to canoe to Tangier, that we would do it. Once we got there, we could reconsider whether going on toward Dar es Salaam by canoe was the wisest choice.

We talked about various aspects of the voyage so far, me stressing the high points and humorous incidents, she enumerating the counterpoints, from use of the Michelin road map to losing the compass and getting lost — twice — in fog.

"And you admitted you were bored," said Barbara, finally nailing down her argument.

Ploughing steadily ahead from point A to point B in a slow-moving kayak did mean a lot of boredom. But I insisted this was one of the prices we had to pay.

I had found that I could put up with solitude and boredom when detained in solitary confinement in South Africa. Spending at least twenty-three hours a day in a small cell, even if only for eight weeks, can be excruciatingly boring and, after a week or two, some detainees screamed to be let out. Most did not — and found ways of coping. My way of coping was what Barbara would later call "your annoying habit of retreating into your head".

"It's all in the mind," I told her. "Just a matter of psychological adjustment to getting from A to B."

"But what's the point of adjusting to an absurd and highly impractical way of getting from A to B?" said Barbara. "Aircraft fly from point A (London) to point B (Dar es Salaam). People generally don't paddle there in kayaks."

By the early hours of the following morning, the die was cast. We would give up the kayak journey and sell *Amandla*, hopefully in the yacht harbour, for enough money to pay our train fares to Gibraltar. There we would plan the next, land-bound, stage of our journey to Dar es Salaam.

It was, for us, a momentous date: Friday, 3 May 1968. A day when everything changed. It was also the very day that the political ferment that had been growing in Paris for weeks finally erupted in the French capital, although we only heard about the "May events" months later.

On a visit to the harbour of Arenys de Mar the following day, we were told that if we wanted to sell our kayak, it would be best to come on the Sunday, when the yachting fraternity tended to be there in numbers.

It was almost time to say goodbye to *Amandla*.

CHAPTER 21

Farewell to *Amandla*, welcome to 3rd-class rail

E arly on Sunday, 5 May 1968, I found a bamboo stave and a small plank in the campsite and scavenged some charcoal from an old fire. I wrote *Se Vende*[56] on the plank with the charcoal, lashed it to the top of the bamboo and put the bamboo into the mast hole in the front of the kayak.

We took out everything except the two lifejackets, the water bottles and the wheeled cradle, and I manoeuvred the now quite light *Amandla* down to the water's edge. The sea was still not very calm, but nowhere near as rough as when we had landed.

I managed to get away without incident and paddled across choppy waters to the harbour entrance and into the harbour, where a number of very posh yachts were tied up. As I paddled among the moored craft, I was called over and, after conversations in a mixture of French, Spanish and German that I did my best to follow, *Amandla* was sold to a young man from the island of Minorca. On Minorca, he said, he had a similar kayak, and she and *Amandla* would make for a good pair.

Barbara and I had decided we could sell our kayak for the equivalent of £18, or 3,000 pesetas, but we decided we would ask for 3,500 to cover our train fares to Gibraltar and some spending money. Unfortunately, I couldn't remember what "half" was in Spanish, the language in which I was asked the price. So I said "*tres mil*" (3,000) when I should have said "*tres mil y media*". Still, we had our basic fare and could head out to our next *poste restante* in the fishing port of Sitges.

That afternoon, as we were packing up our belongings, making up our rucksacks and filling up the large holdall and basket we also carried, we saw *Amandla* leaving the yacht harbour strapped to the

---

56 For Sale

roof of a large Spanish saloon car. There were tears in Barbara's eyes as she watched car and kayak drive off down the road.

"I was really very fond of her," she said.

But I could tell that she was relieved at not having to go back to sea.

The question remained: how were we going to get to Dar es Salaam? Moreover, we had by then promised both sets of parents that we would travel on from Tanzania to Botswana, where we could all meet.

Our parents had met in South Africa and seemed to have got along well, but Barbara's parents had yet to meet me. Their image of their son-in-law would probably not have been helped by my mother's description of me: typically along the lines of, "a very nice boy, but can be irresponsible; thinks he can change the world".

However, that was the least of our worries as we mulled over how we would leave Europe now that the canoe venture was over. We had our hats, our tent, our camping gear and enough money to keep us going for at least a couple of months. And there was always the possibility that we could find some work on Gibraltar.

"If we're getting short in the meantime, we could always sell some blood in Granada," noted Barbara, recalling that several travellers had told us that Granada was where one got the best price for a pint of blood.

One of the people who told us about the selling of blood was a young Englishman camped with his Swedish wife at Arenys de Mar on their way to France. They had travelled third class throughout Spain, they said, on the *trenes de correo* — the mail trains. Definitely better than hitch-hiking, they said, and probably cheaper, since one could sleep on trains and in stations even if it wasn't very comfortable. But they warned us that it was slow and that "people never leave you alone".

We decided to take the train to Algeciras. Then Barbara remembered the old British Post Office van parked alongside Jock's hostel. When Jock was gently trying to persuade us to start a hostel in Tangier, he'd suggested we take the van over to Morocco as temporary accommodation.

Barbara thought this could be the answer. We could take the central route across the Sahara Desert by driving from Morocco to Algeria and then down to Niger and Chad. It was a well-travelled route so, even if we got stuck, there would always be travellers heading either north or south. And once the desert was behind us, it would be relatively easy to travel across to Uganda and Kenya before turning south to Tanzania and Dar es Salaam. As long as we carried enough fuel and water, we should be fine.

I still felt as if I had somehow cheated by not making it at least to Gibraltar and across to Tangier by canoe. But the idea of travelling in a van overland to Dar es Salaam was certainly attractive.

In the meantime, we needed to get to Sitges for our mail and then on to Gibraltar. So, with makeshift rucksacks on our backs, camera and tape recorder slung from neck and shoulders, and carrying a large holdall, a basket and our typewriter between us, we set off. This time there would be no more hitch-hiking; bus and train would be the means of transport.

"We look like a combination of Roma gypsies and rich tourists," Barbara remarked.

We'd seen the Roma on several occasions when hitch-hiking, carrying all they possessed in a large, unwieldy assortment of packages. Similarly burdened, we arrived in Barcelona on a warm, sunny day and booked our train tickets to Sitges and then right through Spain to the far southern coast at Algeciras. With a couple of hours to kill before catching our train, we sat on a bench in a nearby park discussing what the future held for us. It was only after we returned to the railway station that I noticed that Barbara's hat was missing. She had left it hanging on the park bench.

We piled the rest of our belongings onto the train, which was leaving in fifteen minutes, and I ran back to the park, thinking I'd have plenty of time to get back to the train. But when I got to the bench, the hat was gone. And when I arrived, breathless, back at the station, all our

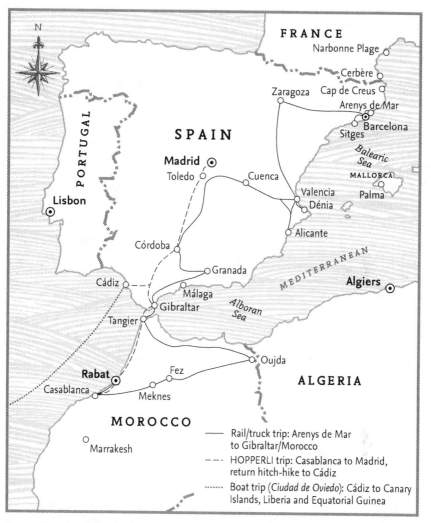

N

FRANCE
Narbonne Plage
Cerbère
Cap de Creus
Zaragoza
Arenys de Mar
Barcelona
Sitges
Balearic Sea
MALLORCA
Palma

PORTUGAL

SPAIN

Madrid
Toledo
Cuenca
Valencia
Dénia

Lisbon

Alicante

Córdoba
Granada
MEDITERRANEAN

Cádiz
Málaga
Algiers
Gibraltar
Alboran Sea
Tangier

Oujda

Rabat
Fez
ALGERIA

Casablanca
Meknes

MOROCCO

Marrakesh

—— Rail/truck trip: Arenys de Mar
to Gibraltar/Morocco

--- HOPPERLI trip: Casablanca to Madrid,
return hitch-hike to Cádiz

······ Boat trip (*Ciudad de Oviedo*): Cádiz to Canary
Islands, Liberia and Equatorial Guinea

Farewell to *Amandla*: the last stages

gear was on the platform beside the open door of the carriage.

Barbara was a short distance up the platform speaking to a railway official. I assumed she had been worried that I wouldn't get back in time and had disembarked. So I started loading our gear back onto the carriage, only to be stopped by an angry exclamation from the railwayman and a shout from Barbara: "Stop! It's the wrong train!"

Out came the bags I had put in and I slammed the door closed as a whistle sounded and the train pulled out.

The train to Sitges, it transpired, was on another platform and was also about to leave. If we ran, we should be able to catch it. We did, and got aboard with no time to spare. As we settled down I did a quick check of our possessions: there was no typewriter. Barbara had put it under the seat in the first train we had boarded and had forgotten about it.

At the next station we clambered out, dumping our possessions next to a bench. I would take the next train back to Barcelona to retrieve my machine and Barbara would wait for me.

It turned out to be a very long wait — seven hours in fact. But, for all the difficulties in language, with several points being lost in translation on a number of occasions, the Spanish railway system came up trumps.

At Barcelona station I was able to explain what had happened and an official immediately got on the telephone. I was told that the typewriter had been found at a remote inland station. It would be returned on the next available train.

That was some three or four hours later. I then had to wait for a train for Sitges to meet up with Barbara at the first station on the line and re-board with all our goods and chattels.

Reunited with the typewriter and one another, we resumed our journey. As the train clacked its way down the line, I pointed out to Barbara that this sort of thing — the loss of a typewriter — would never have happened had we been at sea.

"That might be true," she said. "But compasses apparently get lost at sea, and in storms and fog, people can and do die, and all their possessions go down to the bottom."

I thought it best not to argue.

That night we got into Sitges and treated ourselves to a bed in a small pension. The next morning we strolled through what was still a delightful Spanish fishing village, though the marks of tourist colonialism were already evident: "Tea like mother makes it," read one sign; "Real English Fish and Chips," read another, bearing a Union Jack.

"Here comes Tossa de Mar," said Barbara.

We picked up our mail, wrote some replies, and decided that we would stop off along the route whenever we could, to experience something more of Spain. As the couple in Arenys de Mar had said, we could travel at night, sleeping on trains or in stations, and spend some time in places along the way during the day. Having experienced the Crusader fortress of Aigues-Mortes, I wanted to see the Alhambra Palace and old Granada, the stronghold of the Muslim emirs who had ruled over the Iberian Peninsula for more than 700 years.

All that remained was to catch a bus back to Barcelona and book our tickets. At the railway station we found that there was a *tren de correo* that could take us very cheaply, in third class, across a large area of Spain, via Valencia and Alicante, to Granada. We could stop where we wished and had only to rely on each mail train going our way. It was a sort of early Eurail pass. Finally, from Granada it would be about four hours to Algeciras and La Línea, and from there a walk across the airport runway to Gibraltar. The only problem was that we had set as our next *poste restante* the coastal town of Dénia, to which there was no rail connection. We would have to find our way there by other means.

CHAPTER 22

No man is an island

We soon discovered that a bus travelled regularly to Dénia and back from Valencia. So in Sitges we boarded the train bound for Valencia and began a slow, but fascinating, rail ride through days and nights.

Late one night we were stranded with a large group of peasant conscripts to the army somewhere on a secondary railway line south of Madrid. It was quite chilly and we had crowded into the railway waiting room. It turned out to have tremendous acoustics, so when a couple of the lads began to sing, we recorded them. The others joined in — a spontaneous mass choir.

They sang; we recorded. We played the recording to them and they expressed their appreciation. Then they sang again and we played the recording back again. With considerable mime and laughter, we all talked. The hours flew by. There were fond farewell scenes when their train finally arrived and we wished them *"buen viaje"*. That impromptu concert in the middle of nowhere was one of the highlights of our brief, culturally kaleidoscopic journey back to the Rock, both on and off the rails.

Our train to Valencia eventually turned up and we piled in with the other passengers who, like most on that long train journey, tended to carry drawstring bags and numerous boxes tied with string.

Arriving in Valencia mid-morning, we discovered that we would have to wait overnight for the bus to Dénia, so we booked into a local pension. Walking around town that evening, we were fortunate to meet a Mexican-American naval petty officer, Cal, from Texas, on shore leave from a Mediterranean Fleet supply ship in the harbour. Noticing my hat, he struck up a conversation that ended with an unexpected culinary treat. He spoke fluent Spanish and at a nearby restaurant introduced

158

us to a local speciality — *riñones al jerez*.[57] Julio, the restaurant's *jefe*,[58] claimed, with apparent justification, that his *riñones* dish was the finest in the world. Judging by the number of orders, we were in no position to contradict him. And it was, indeed, delicious.

The following morning we caught the bus to Dénia, where another helpful bus driver saw us to a very pleasant campsite called Los Pinos. It was right on the coast and, in accordance with its name, was dotted with pine trees that provided shade to caravans and tents. Despite lingering feelings of guilt at having given up the kayak venture, I was starting to enjoy myself. Barbara was totally in her element, unaware that I still had misgivings. During a particularly interesting and animated conversation with Henk and Jannie, a Dutch couple from Rotterdam who were camped beside us, she said, "Apart from that one fisherman, we never met anyone out on the water."

It brought home to me then quite how boring much of the sea canoeing had been. I also realised how superficial our contacts were while on the water, even in the canals and rivers: nodding, hat-doffing acquaintances with bargee families; pleasantries exchanged with lock-keepers and stallholders as we passed through. Only in Aigues-Mortes, where we had spent some time, had we really got to know something about the people. And there was that fortuitous meeting in Saint-Gilles that educated us about wine.

After nearly a week in Dénia, where we caught up on and replied to post from our parents, we were back in Valencia for what we assumed would be a quick trip to Alicante. But nobody seemed too sure when the train would arrive at its destination. The standard response to queries about routes and arrivals was a perfunctory, "*No sé*",[59] yet

---

57 lamb kidneys in a sherry sauce
58 manager
59 "Don't know"

this seemed not to concern our fellow passengers. They shrugged, smiled, and seemed perfectly content that they would eventually get to where they were going.

With our previous experience of the ten-seater wooden benches on the third-class *trenes de correo*, we had our sleeping bags ready as padding when we boarded and settled in for our trip to Alicante. On the bench opposite us sat a stern-faced woman with her arm in plaster and a sling, trying, without success, to encourage her seven- or eight-year-old son to sit beside her. He shouted. He jeered. He jumped up on the seat and bumped into other passengers, who merely shrugged. The mother, obviously noticing that we were foreign, gestured disapprovingly at my hat and then, stroking her own chin, indicated that I should shave my beard. After a while I thought it best to remove myself, so I made my way to the toilet at the end of the carriage.

On my way back I had to force myself through a scrum of passengers who were clustered around the benches where Barbara was sitting, clutching the tape recorder. Heads leaned over the benches before and behind.

The grim-faced woman — Hatchet Face, as I came to call her — gestured imperiously that I should take my seat. As I sat down Barbara whispered to me that she had taken out the recorder to start a tape to her parents and that the woman sitting opposite had recognised it as a recording machine. She had immediately insisted that her son be recorded singing.

I turned to the woman. "*Canta?*"[60] I said, using one of the few words in my Spanish vocabulary.

"*Sí, canta magníficamente,*"[61] she announced loudly to the carriage as a whole.

---

60 "Sing?"
61 "Yes, he sings magnificently."

On hearing this, the scrum of passengers began several animated conversations that seemed to be about singing.

Hatchet Face paid no attention to the hubbub. Having apparently decided that my fractured Spanish was inadequate, she addressed us in only slightly less fractured English and indicated that we should, after recording her son, take both the boy and the recording to England, where he would become famous.

She seemed most upset when I told her that we were not heading to England, but to Africa — to Dar es Salaam.

Nonetheless, she demanded that we record the magnificent voice of her son. The boy was not interested, leaping up and down at the window. But Hatchet Face grabbed him by the arm and placed him in front of me and the tape recorder. He stuck out his tongue and sneered at me. Then, noticing that he was the centre of attention, he cleared his throat. I readied the microphone. And he sang. Maybe not magnificently, but beautifully. Twice.

There were compliments by our fellow passengers and discussions ensued about songs and music. We were acknowledged, despite our very peripheral involvement in the performance. The boy, in the meantime, swaggered and jumped about, ignored for the most part. Fortunately, somewhere along the line he and his mother departed and we were left in relative peace, having made an unspoken agreement to keep the tape recorder out of sight unless there was something — or someone — we really wanted to record.

The train clicked and clacked its way beyond Alicante and took us slowly past the slate-grey, snow-capped Sierra Nevada on what turned out to be a sixteen-hour journey. It was a stunning scene. When day broke, high up on the sandstone cliff faces, we could see the famous white-washed, sandstone cave homes, the *casa cuevas*, some dating back at least as far as the Arab invasion of Iberia in the eighth century. But most of these Hobbit-like warrens were excavated by peasant farmers in the eighteenth century — perfect insulation in a quite extreme climate. We adopted the laid-back approach of the other passengers as the train stopped and started, never moving at any great pace. We finally pulled into Granada near midnight.

There would be no sleeping on the station; we would find a good, cheap pension in one of the old quarters and spend the next few days exploring a city that had been one of the wealthiest in medieval Europe. In the wake of the armies of the largely secular Umayyad dynasty that crossed from Africa through the Strait of Gibraltar some 1,300 years earlier had come great art, architecture and medical knowledge. Granada was a centre of scholarship and religious tolerance as well as great wealth. It fell to Christian armies in 1492, the year that Christopher Columbus set sail from a port to the east of Cádiz, to "discover" the Americas. It was also the year that the Spanish Inquisition ordered all Jews and Muslims to convert to Christianity or leave Spain.

Granada did not disappoint. The rich and complex history was everywhere in evidence: in the swarthy complexions of many people, in the architecture and, above all, in Flamenco. This was the natural home of the singing, guitar-playing and hand-clapping dance form that has its roots in North African Islamic and Jewish traditions as well as the music of the Roma, who tend today to lay sole claim to it. They survived the expulsion of the Jews and Muslims, as they had elsewhere in Europe, simply by adapting to the newly dominant religion while preserving their own cultural beliefs and practices — even their language.

The ancient city was something of a mental turning point for me. It drove home the advantage Barbara kept stressing, of travelling on land and, therefore, among people — of listening and learning. Even before we reached the airport runway that marks the entrance to Gibraltar, I no longer felt as remorseful about abandoning *Amandla* and the sea.

CHAPTER 23

Heading south in a converted British Post Office van

Jock was happy to see us, and readily agreed to us using the pink Post Office van for our trans-African safari. It was a gift, he said, but he would accept a minimum contribution of around £10 to the hostel fund.

An American traveller staying at the hostel — Dougie (Douglas Neil) MacDonald — was equally pleased to meet us, for different reasons. Dougie, an ebullient young refugee from the Bible Belt, had bought a Triumph 250cc motorcycle and wanted to take it down through Africa with a "base vehicle". The ex-GPO van we intended travelling in was an obvious candidate. It had kitchen and cupboard space inside, including, Barbara gleefully noted, a two-ring gas stove. There was also a large open "sleeping" space in the middle. The motorcycle could be carried in there and taken out at night to be parked alongside the tent in which Dougie would sleep. The motorcycle could provide emergency transport should that be necessary.

So Douglas, Barbara and I, with assistance from Jock and Ken, began preparing the van for its great journey. Jock was particularly helpful, providing, from his "contacts", grey and black paint to change the livery of the van. Years earlier, he had himself travelled overland from Morocco to Nairobi in Kenya, and he provided useful advice and maps. Doug, who knew more about engines than we did, checked out the mechanics, along with Ken.

We also did a fair amount of research and planned a route that would take us from Tangier to the Algerian border at Oujda. From there we would follow the coast to Algiers to stock up on extra fuel and water before driving the nearly 900 kilometres to El Ménia, an oasis town in the Sahara Desert. There, we would refuel before getting

14/6/68 GREETINGS, FOLKS, AFTER
5 DAYS HERE WE FINALLY MOVE OUT

Oujda, home to campers

to the border of Niger at In Guezzam, along what Jock referred to as the "Hogarth Line". Once we crossed to Agadez we would have another 3,000 kilometres to go to Kampala in Uganda, then on to Nairobi and, finally, down to Dar es Salaam. It would be about 8,000 kilometres. We thought we could do it in about three weeks — a far cry from the pace of the kayak.

The vehicle was sound, ready — we were sure — to take on at least 10,000 kilometres without too many problems. But although it carried English licence plates, it was not registered anywhere, was not insured and, according to its single piece of official paper, belonged to Captain W. B. Brown. I duly typed up a sale and ownership agreement, complete with TocH stamps from the hostel, and we considered ourselves ready to roll. There was an emotional farewell from Jock, his assistant at the hostel, Isabel, and Ken when we finally readied ourselves to depart.

164

"Look after yourselves," Jock said.

It was the last time we saw him, and we did not hear from him again.

When we trundled down to the harbour to catch the ferry we were shocked to find that our vehicle was, in colouring, a land-based replica of the British warships anchored in the bay; the black and grey paint had obviously come from the naval base. But there were no questions as we drove aboard the ferry and nobody queried the papers or the motorcycle.

We were on our way.

We stopped over that night near a village in the Atlas Mountains. When we opened the back doors of the van in the morning (with Doug still asleep in the tent below), we were taken aback to find twenty children sitting on the ground, staring up at us. Then a woman appeared, carrying a dish of goat's milk as a welcome gift. We thanked her and, when several men approached, we explained as best we could that we had only stopped overnight and would soon be on our way. They issued the customary invitation to stay and, when we gracefully declined, wished us well. After a breakfast that included the goat's milk, we set off for Oujda and the border.

We passed a sign advertising "Camping — Oujda", but we had no intention of stopping. It was little over 500 kilometres to Algiers from the border and we thought we should make it to the Algerian capital by nightfall. When we got to the border, however, we were told that Doug and Barbara were acceptable, but I was not welcome. This had nothing to do with my hat. It transpired that, because I had listed my occupation on the passport as "journalist", I was *persona non grata*. I protested. I was not working as a journalist, I pointed out. I was merely a traveller and, besides, the organisation to which I was affiliated, the African National Congress (ANC) of South Africa, had good relations with the Algerian government. In fact, the ANC had an office in Algiers.

What we were not aware of was that there had been considerable political upheaval in Algeria. Ahmed Ben Bella, whom we in the ANC had loudly hailed, had not only been deposed as president in 1965, but was then under house arrest. Also the tremors of the "May events" in Paris — of which we were also completely unaware — had made regimes everywhere rather wary, especially of journalists.

So it was that the battleship grey ex-GPO van and its three occupants became residents of Camping — Oujda. Every day for a week, we would drive out of the campsite to the border to find out if I had been cleared to enter. It was a stonewall situation. Then, on the morning of 15 June 1968, a sand-blasted, mud-bedecked Land Rover entered the camp: three Hollanders had just made the crossing and they brought bad news. The rains, south of Algeria, had come early and the road into Niger was impassable.

In those days before the trans-Saharan highway, this could mean waiting two or three months before being able to cross. And in our vehicle, without four-wheel drive, we would need dry weather roads. We called a meeting and decided that our best choice would be to drive back to Casablanca and try to find a ship that could take us around the western bulge of Africa, past the Sahara, to somewhere like Senegal.

We drove out of Oujda on Sunday, 16 June, and did not stop at Fez, Meknes or anywhere else along the route. We covered the 600 or so kilometres to Casablanca as quickly as possible and that evening pulled in to the city's inappropriately named "Camping Oasis". The next two days were spent largely down at the harbour, talking to shipping agents, officials from shipping companies, captains and crews. It seemed there was a good prospect of a ship sailing to Senegal. But we might need a visa.

Doug was more fortunate. He found an American tanker heading for Houston, Texas, and the captain was prepared to take his motorcycle aboard. As he was due back at university in a couple of months, he decided to fly back to New York and travel down to Texas to pick up the bike.

166

In the meantime, Barbara and I drove to Rabat to find out whether, as Irish citizens, we needed a visa for Senegal. It seemed that nobody at the Senegalese Embassy had ever heard of Ireland. My explanation that it was "*a côté de la Grand Bretagne*"[62] solicited the suggestion: "*Les Pays-Bas?*" I explained that "les Pays-Bas" was Holland, in the Low Countries.

In the end, to be on the safe side, we paid for a visa for Senegal and drove back to Casablanca, only to find out that it would be two months before the next ship sailed for Senegal. And it was not certain that it would take us and our van.

Day after day we trudged around, pleading, arguing, offering to work our passages. Then, in mid-July, in the sweltering heat of a Moroccan summer, a Swedish journalist arrived in Camping Oasis. Until then the only resident we had made contact with was a draft dodger from both the Swiss and Austrian armies — Werner. Werner slept under the counter of the campsite bar and was the goalkeeper for the local soccer team. Every morning he would come to the van, chessboard under his arm, and yell out in German, "Terry, *willst du schach spielen?*"[63] I think, like several mediocre chess players in my experience, he enjoyed playing against me, because, like them, he always won.

Unlike Werner, the Swede spoke English, did not want to play chess, and that night was perhaps not quite as appalled as we were to hear that we were completely unaware of "Paris '68": of the demonstrations, the barricades, the "people's university" at the Sorbonne. He had covered the whole uprising as a photo-journalist and was taking a break in Morocco.

"You should have been there," he enthused.

Here we were, drifting in a self-imposed bubble, surrounded by

---

62 "next to Great Britain"
63 "Terry, do you want to play chess?"

history, but oblivious to it. If sedate, organised, affluent and apparently bourgeois Paris could suddenly erupt in that fashion, then what about South Africa? Victory in Vietnam was also certain. Change was coming — and faster than anyone might have imagined. Here was evidence of the promise of the future, confirmation of the youthful optimism of the Sixties.

Barbara and I agreed: we would not "hang around" Casablanca in the hope of a ship taking us to Senegal in a couple of months. We would get moving.

But how?

One of the problems we had come up against when talking to shipping agents was the size of our van. It did seem that size counted, certainly in terms of the cost of shipping. We also discovered that it was cheaper to ship the van down the west coast of Africa from Las Palmas in the Canary Islands. But how to get there in the first place? One of the shipping agents had also suggested that we should try Cádiz in southern Spain, where, he had heard, a very inexpensive shipping ran down the west coast.

Werner came to the rescue: it turned out he owned a small Citroën 2CV car with a roll-down canvas roof. These vehicles were incredible. They had independent suspension and were extremely basic and cheap to run. There was not even a fuel gauge, merely a dipstick into the fuel tank, but the cars were said to be able to go anywhere extremely cheaply — if rather slowly. Werner wanted to be rid of the car, which he had dubbed "HOPPERLI". The name was painted on the grey, corrugated back, along with a large Swiss flag.

Werner couldn't drive, and the two companions — both drivers — who had accompanied him from Austria to Casablanca, had deserted him when he decided to stay. The car was in perfect condition, having been fully serviced and checked out at a local service station.

"It's obvious," said Werner. "You should sell your van and buy my HOPPERLI."

We couldn't fault his logic.

Since we had already had a couple of unsolicited offers for the van from dealers in Casablanca, we thought we should shop around for the best deal. Big mistake. Instead of taking the first good offer, we drove around to a couple of other dealers who offered substantially less. And when we got back to the first dealer, the original deal no longer applied: he offered even less than the others. Here was the classic example of a cartel in operation.

Instead of the hefty profit we thought we would make, we ended up selling the van for little more than we paid Werner for HOPPERLI. But although we couldn't cook, eat or camp in it, the Citroën was a much better bet to get us across Africa. We still had our tent and all our camping gear and, besides, it would cost a great deal less to ship the car.

So we piled all our belongings — including tent, anoraks, clothing, extra fuel tanks and other paraphernalia — into the back of this remarkably efficient tin can on wheels. Then, slowly but surely, with the independent suspension to keep us comfortable, we headed back to Tangier, back to the ferry and back to Algeciras. From there it was a left turn onto the road to Cádiz, one-time home of the fabulous Spanish treasure fleets and probably Europe's oldest city.

CHAPTER 24

A car called HOPPERLI & the fate of the hat

The Phoenicians, the Romans, the Umayyad "Moors" — for over 3,000 years, Cádiz had been their city. Traces of this heritage remained but, to our continuing regret, we did not experience the city's rich antiquity. We headed straight to the harbour and discovered that there was indeed a ship — in fact two ships, alternating with one another — sailing every three weeks or so from Cádiz, via Las Palmas and Monrovia, to Equatorial Guinea. There was a flat fare, whether one embarked from Bilbao in northern Spain or Cádiz, to either Santa Isabel (Malabo) on the island of Fernando Po (Bioko Norte) or Bata on the Rio Muni (Bioko) mainland.

Equatorial Guinea is essentially one small island in the Bight of Biafra and a sliver of mainland sandwiched between Cameroon and Gabon, which, in October 1968, was to gain its independence from Spain. In the meantime, the colonial supply ships continued to run and we could catch a third-class ride on one of them.

It was a two-week journey, for £15 a head, all found, including bed and board, and £15 for the car. We had no idea what that meant, and we knew nothing about our destination, which was at that stage the last Spanish colonial outpost in Africa, with the exception of Ceuta and Melilla. As it turned out, very few people (including those working in banks and the postal authorities) were that conversant with Equatorial Guinea either, something that was to cause us considerable problems.

But our passport and our papers (I had created another typewritten set to cover our purchase of HOPPERLI from Werner) were apparently in order. The only problem was that tickets for the voyage, along with a visa for entry into Equatorial Guinea, could only be obtained in Madrid. We would have to drive the approximately 650 kilometres to the Spanish capital, via two historic Andalusian cities — Seville

Madrid: city to the hat and source of a newfound freedom

and Córdoba. It would be fully three weeks before the next supply ship, the *Ciudad de Oviedo*, would sail from Cádiz. We would have plenty of time to pick up our tickets and visa.

At that stage, poring over the maps we had got from Jock and acquired along the way, we were determined not to leave anything to chance. The idea was to drive directly to Madrid, and then return slowly to Cádiz, perhaps calling in at Seville and Córdoba. We also made a pledge that we would pick up every hitch-hiker we could accommodate.

Once we and HOPPERLI disembarked at Bata, we would drive the 500 kilometres to the Cameroonian capital of Yaoundé, where we would spend some time planning the next stage of the journey. If need be, we would take our time and set up fuel drops along the 3,500-kilometre route to Kampala in Uganda. From there on, it seemed fairly straightforward: another 650 kilometres on a good, well-used road to Nairobi, and then south for another 825 kilometres to Dar es Salaam.

We would soon be heading "home" to southern Africa and, perhaps for the first time in ages, we were feeling very relaxed. With the canvas cartop down and my hat given pride of place on a pile of goods at the very back, we started on our slow but steady way to the Spanish capital.

We spent the night at a nondescript campsite and before sunrise were on our way again, with a map of the Spanish capital in hand. By mid-morning we found ourselves in one of the main thoroughfares near the shipping office where we had been told to get our visa, our tickets and a cargo note for HOPPERLI. I pulled into a parking spot, alongside bus stop 18.

"Perhaps I should stay," said Barbara.

When I didn't answer, she decided to join me. So we pulled up the canvas top (it was held to the ridge of the windscreen by two simple clips) and locked the doors. Then I remembered that my hat was still inside, at the back. Never mind, we would be gone only fifteen or twenty minutes. In high spirits, we crossed the road and made our way to the address we had been given.

Not only did we find it without any problem, but there was no-one else there and the service was impeccable. In minutes we had a visa stamp in our passport and tickets for ourselves and HOPPERLI from Cádiz to Bata.

That night we would celebrate. At a nearby supermarket I bought a good bottle of Cava, the Spanish sparkling wine, while Barbara laid in supplies for what we saw as our "farewell to Europe" dinner. Packages in hand, we were coming down some steps, laughing, when I looked across to where HOPPERLI had been parked.

There was nothing. An open space. It was gone.

"Are you sure this is the right place?" Barbara asked.

We both knew it was.

"Perhaps the police have towed it away," she added desperately.

But we knew they hadn't.

I felt my head, and remembered. "My hat was in the car!" I said.

"Never mind your hat — everything we own was in there!" said Barbara.

That wasn't strictly true. We had the clothes we stood up in, such as they were, our passport, our tickets, our recent purchases and, most importantly, what remained of our money. The obvious next stop had to be the police station. There was one just across the way. Our car had been stolen almost within sight of the police.

Even with the aid of a quite competent interpreter, it was one of the most frustrating experiences either of us had ever endured. The police were happy to make a note of the theft, but were not prepared to do anything about it; instead they kept insisting that we fill in forms for insurance for everything missing.

Perhaps understandably, they could not conceive that we did not have insurance, that all we wanted was our car back and that if they moved fast, they should be able to find it before it disappeared for good. Could they not, by radio, notify all units — there seemed to be no shortage of police — to look out for what must be one of the most recognisable cars anywhere, with great white capital letters across the back spelling HOPPERLI, accompanied by a large Swiss flag?

The officers shrugged; the Guardia in the background rolled their eyes. Clearly we were mad. Again they pressed a claims form on us. We were getting nowhere and perhaps it was wisest not to explain in too much detail about how we came to have no insurance. They might even conclude that we had stolen the car. So we made a hasty retreat.

The Irish Embassy might provide some help, although we remembered the warning delivered in London about Ireland not having many diplomatic representatives abroad. But we were eventually directed to a block of apartments in central Madrid, that housed the decidedly insalubrious headquarters of the Embassy of the Republic of Ireland, with its staff of two — an ambassador and a secretary. The ambassador was away in Bilbao for a sitting of the Spanish Parliament. A young secretary, Michael Lillas, later to become a major figure in Irish foreign affairs, welcomed us and cleared up our confusion about the lack of action on the part of the police.

There was, it seemed, an understanding between the police and the thieves that was supposed to keep everybody happy, including the tourists. The only losers were the insurance companies. The reason the police were so keen to have us list stolen goods, at whatever figure we wished to claim, was in order to help us gain maximum recompense. The thieves would not be interested in the car — there was no stolen car market in Spain — but would make off with the contents of the vehicle. That would keep them happy and out of perhaps more destructive or dangerous mischief, which, in turn, would mean an easier life for the police.

It all made sense. And, said Michael Lillas, since we had two weeks before our ship was scheduled to leave Cádiz, we should tour the back streets of the capital. There was every likelihood that we would find the car. Feeling slightly hopeful as we left the building, I harboured thoughts of not only seeing the car again, but of spotting someone wearing my hat — THE hat. There would be no politely negotiated price and I would get it back.

I suddenly felt extremely vulnerable without my hat. My vengeful thoughts were interrupted by Barbara pointing out that we still had our shopping with us.

"What do we do with all this?" she asked. "Take it back?"

"I guess so," I said.

So we walked back to the supermarket and explained that our car had been stolen, that the police had been notified. The manager commiserated and took back the olive oil, the pasta and the Cava. We decided to keep the salami and the bread: we were going to have to eat as cheaply as possible as we started our grand search.

Since we were in the area, we also called in at the shipping office and explained what had happened. The assistant behind the counter threw up his hands and, with a look of what I thought was sympathetic resignation, announced that he would refund the £15 equivalent for the car. If — and he looked very doubtful — *if* the car was found, there would be no problem: there would still be room aboard and he would re-issue the cargo note for HOPPERLI.

We accepted his kind offer. Then, after spending several hours walking through some of the seedier streets and planning the routes we would take in coming days, we asked at a little café/bar about suitable — clean and cheap — places to stay. The *jefe*, having heard the tale of woe told to him in impoverished Spanish, peppered with bad French and much gesticulation, said there was only one place — a pension just down the street. It was both *muy limpio*[64] and *muy barato*.[65] I also got the impression that he was warning us to be on our best behaviour, suggesting that the landlady did not take kindly to any funny business.

After buying a couple of toothbrushes, toothpaste, soap and a razor, we turned up at the pension in the late afternoon. After the warning from the *jefe* of the café/bar down the road, we were not taken aback when we first saw the landlady: a small, black-garbed widow whose strong voice and piercing eyes seemed to belie the age signalled by her stoop and her craggy, wrinkled face. When she spoke, her gnarled hands fluttered, birdlike, but there was more of the raptor than the robin about her.

She eyed us with suspicion that bordered on hostility. But she listened attentively as we painstakingly explained our predicament. She then quoted an amount per night that was astonishingly cheap. It seemed this room was the only low-budget option available in her first-floor rooming house.

"*Pero, no hay ventana,*"[66] she said.

I didn't know what *ventana* meant. Vent? Aircon? Unlikely. But if it was clean and reasonably comfortable, what did it matter?

"That's fine," I replied and she signalled us to follow her.

---

64 very clean
65 very cheap
66 "But there is no window."

She pointed out the communal bathroom and toilet that was minimalist and clean-scrubbed. Then she opened a single door alongside the stairwell on the way to the entrance, reached in and switched on a light.

That was when I added "window" to my limited Spanish vocabulary: *ventana*. There was no window. Only, high up on the wall, overlooking the stairwell, an opening: the single apparent provision for ventilation. It was effectively a converted cupboard. But the bed, which was against the wall and had stopped the door from opening fully, was made up with crisp white sheets and there were two pillows looking similarly well laundered.

"*Muy bien, gracias,*"[67] I said in what I hoped was a reasonable Spanish accent.

The landlady's expression never changed, but one hand fluttered out. "*Dinero, por una noche,*"[68] she said.

Obviously if we did not meet her standards, we would be out after one night.

We weren't overly concerned about the fact that we had no way of telling the time and no natural light to provide any indication of whether it was day or night. For as long as I could remember, I had been able to set my mind to wake at certain times. It was what Barbara referred to as my "biological clock". In any event, we faced long days of walking if we couldn't quickly find the car and would invariably be very early to bed, so we would be unlikely to oversleep.

But there was also the problem of clothes. In the heat of summer, we had discovered that we could wash our T-shirts and underwear, hang them up and they would be dry by morning. But we clearly needed something more. On the second day, an answer presented itself as we passed a large department store. It was advertising a massive sale in

---

67 "Very good, thanks."
68 "Money, for one night."

two days' time. Given that Spain in those days was extremely cheap by British and French standards, a cut-price sale was not to be missed.

On the morning of the sale, we were up and about before 6 a.m., and without even stopping at the café on the corner for our usual coffee and churros[69] we headed for the store, expecting to be first at the doors. We were wrong. Our landlady was not there, but she seemed to have been cloned: there were at least twenty stooped, black-garbed and variously wrinkled women, several gabbling frantically to one another, others looking steely and determined.

There seemed to be no idea of a queue, more a continuous jostle around the doors of the store. We found ourselves manoeuvred further back as still more similarly garbed women arrived. Within an hour we were in a sea of chattering, jostling women who seemed to possess elbows like steel levers. I stood my ground and held onto Barbara who was of similar height to most of the women, but was constantly being pulled back further from the doors by this black tide.

And then the doors opened. Pandemonium.

Our decisions had already been made; we knew what we should try to buy and the limit of our budget. We would head separately for the different departments and meet outside once the purchases were made.

Barbara disappeared into the maelstrom and I made my way to the menswear section, where, as the first man to arrive, I managed to buy a pair of black leather shoes, three pairs of socks, two changes of underwear, two shirts (one light blue, the other white with blue pinstripe), and a pair of — like the shirts, drip-dry — trousers with a hanger that clamped the legs to maintain the creases. To top it off — a dark blue tie. We were going to have to hitch-hike in Spain, after all.

I then joined a minor scrum and managed to buy a large zip-top shoulder bag to carry our worldly goods. Then it was outside to wait for Barbara, who eventually appeared, having managed to buy

---

69 fried-dough pastry rolled in sugar

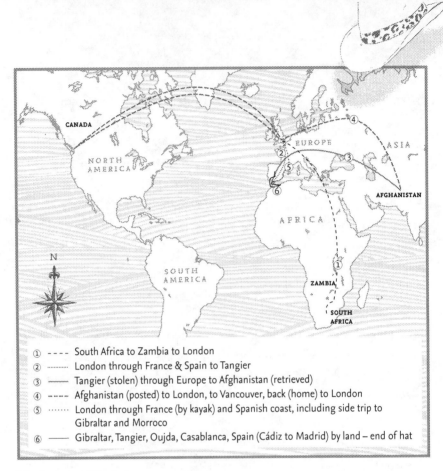

① - - - - South Africa to Zambia to London
② .... London through France & Spain to Tangier
③ ———— Tangier (stolen) through Europe to Afghanistan (retrieved)
④ -- -- -- Afghanistan (posted) to London, to Vancouver, back (home) to London
⑤ .... London through France (by kayak) and Spanish coast, including side trip to
           Gibraltar and Morroco
⑥ ———— Gibraltar, Tangier, Oujda, Casablanca, Spain (Cádiz to Madrid) by land – end of hat

The journey of the hat

two skirts, two blouses, underwear and a pair of fashionable leather sandals. We added up the cost: an unbelievable £6. Then it was back to our cupboard and, again, out into the back streets of Madrid.

We found a number of obviously stolen or otherwise abandoned vehicles as we ticked off the areas covered on our city map. Among them was a Citroën DS19, a car that had fascinated me with its pneumatic suspension. This one was covered in the dust of many months of neglect. Inscribed in the dust on the rear window were the words "*Estoy Robado*".[70] All it probably required to get it going again would be a battery.

---

70 "I Am Stolen"

Even as that thought crossed my mind, Barbara stated firmly, "Don't even think about it."

If I was that obvious, it was just as well I never became a car thief.

Most days, after about six hours of trudging through streets and alleyways, we would make our way back toward the centre of town, where we would sit on the lawns outside the famous Prado Museum and eat our lunch. Here, right before us, was one of the greatest art collections in the world: Goya, El Greco, Velázquez, the nightmarish paintings of Hieronymus Bosch and so much more. But we had no time to spare and, apart from anything else, there was an entry fee.

By the end of the ninth day, we came to the conclusion that we would not find HOPPERLI — or my hat. And because of our previous experiences of hitch-hiking in Spain, we knew we would need to leave plenty of time to get to Cádiz.

We bade our landlady farewell on the morning of the tenth day, receiving a nod in return, and made our way to the Irish Embassy. There we handed over the car keys to Michael Lillas. As the secretary at the embassy he had a bicycle to get around Madrid. Should the 2CV turn up, we said, "she's yours". Then, dressed in our newfound finery, we caught a bus to the outskirts of the city and stood at the side of the road to Seville.

I realised — and bemoaned the fact — that this was the first hitch-hiking trip I had made without my hat since the day I bought it more than five years earlier.

Barbara noted sympathetically: "Maybe it wouldn't go with the way you're dressed."

I had to concede that, sartorially, she had a point. And she was also correct in maintaining that we looked as if our Mercedes had broken down just around the corner.

As we stood at the roadside on that sunny day in late July, with all we owned on our backs and a clear road ahead, Barbara suddenly remarked, "You know, I don't think we'll ever feel as free as this again."

Epilogue

We reached Cádiz without further mishap and boarded the *Ciudad de Oviedo* in the first week of August. Our sea voyage to Equatorial Guinea, via the Canary Islands and the Liberian port capital of Monrovia, would take a fortnight. When we set off from Cádiz, we estimated that we would reach Dar es Salaam within a month or six weeks. From Fernando Po (now Bioko Norte), an island province of Equatorial Guinea, our plan was to travel overland from Yaoundé in Cameroon across the continent to Kampala in Uganda, Nairobi, and then on to Dar.

Our voyage in third class aboard the *Ciudad de Oviedo* was an eye-opener about the realities of Franco's Spain and Spanish colonial attitudes. We travelled in the modern equivalent of steerage with three Guineans and a group of young Spanish naval conscripts. The crew and "upper class" passengers were frankly racist toward the Guineans and arrogant, or at best patronising, to the young, peasant conscripts. A "black Guardia" (political police) captain, apparently booked in first class, strutted about pompously. Even the ship's officers displayed a servile attitude to the man.

When we arrived in the beautiful natural harbour of Santa Isabel (now Malabo), formed by a long-extinct, sea-breached volcanic crater, we intended to stay for no more than a day or two. There was certainly no intention to wait around for Independence Day, scheduled for 12 October. Our plan was to find out as much as we could about any overland route, and as quickly as possible. We would then book a flight across the bay to Douala in Cameroon and take the single rail link to Yaoundé, the capital. There we would be able to obtain whatever visas were necessary and finalise plans for the overland safari.

A day after arriving in Santa Isabel, we booked our flight to Douala, having found out very little about the mainland. Then it was a long and

10 10 48 HELLO FOLKS — YOUR
LETTERS OF THE 30th
N.º 2.- GUINEA ECUATORIAL ← THE 2ND RECEIVED
Muelle antiguo

POR AVION

CORREOS 10

A breached volcanic crater: Santa Isabel (Malabo) harbour

rickety railway ride up to the plateau and Yaoundé, only to discover that there was little or no overland transport. In fact, because of instability in the region, it was recommended that travellers stay put. Barbara's point A to point B argument came fully into force: return to point A, Santa Isabel on Fernando Po, the cheapest place to stay, and buy an airline ticket to point B.

Point B turned out to be, not Dar, the destination that had been our lodestar all these months, but Ndola, Zambia, where I had worked before and might have the prospect of a job. And so began a near three-month comedy of errors, not really of our making.

In the first place, even as late as 1968, the world was not yet the village it has become. Outside of the immediate vicinity of Equatorial Guinea, it was as if the country simply did not exist. This ignorance applied not only to individuals, but to institutions like banks and post offices. (Of course, this was before the discovery of copious quantities of oil and gas in the country.) We discovered this to our cost when we tried to have the last of our savings sent in a bank draft, by post, from London to Santa Isabel. It would be a long wait.

The cheapest place for us to stay in Santa Isabel was a room in the Hotel Flores, where a great overhead fan kept the mosquitoes at bay. But, having paid for lodgings, we had no money for board. We solved this problem by living on bananas filched from plantations along the roadway to the airport.

This was the time of the Biafra War and emergency airlifts, which at least provided material for news and features that I could sell. But since there was only one public telephone in Santa Isabel — a radio link patched through Madrid — and an erratic telex service through the post office, it was extremely difficult, if not impossible, to cover "hot" news. I managed to send some features to publications in Britain by post. However, since we assumed we would soon be in Zambia, I informed publications I sold to (there were very few) that I would contact them when I reached Zambia and they could then pay me. But the weeks ran into months and I lost 20 kilograms (44 pounds) in weight. Barbara, on the other hand, lost about two.

In the meantime, we were the only foreigners — and I the only journalist — present at the extraordinarily low-key independence ceremony on 12 October 1968. There was no celebration. A Spanish naval unit in dress whites presented arms as the Spanish flag was lowered to boos from the crowd of several hundred Guineans — who cheered when the new nation's flag went up. That was it. The sailors and the officers marched off to the harbour and to the warship in the bay; we and a group of Guineans then wandered down the hill to a couple of the back-street bars in Santa Isabel town to toast the end of Spanish rule.

The bank draft from London did eventually arrive — after more than two months — having been redirected from Guinea and then Guinea-Bissau. By this time, having used up our money to eke out an existence, we were again £25 short of the airfare. It looked like we had no alternative but to return to Europe and London. Fortunately we were saved from such ignominy by an Irish friend, Alfie Scott, and his Scottish wife, Sheila, whom we had met on Fernando Po. They lent us the balance, which we later paid back from Zambia, and were finally able to fly out.

It should have been a simple one-day journey from Santa Isabel to Douala, and Douala to Kinshasa, capital of Zaire (now the Democratic Republic of Congo/DRC), with a change of plane to Ndola. But political machinations outside our control, airline bureaucracy and our embarrassment at having to rely on the hospitality of friends turned it into a ten-day ordeal.

At the same time we were leaving Malabo, Zaire's exiled opposition leader, Pierre Mulele, was lured across the Congo River from Brazzaville, capital of the Republic of Congo, to Kinshasa with a promise of amnesty. He was apparently killed in a gruesome way as we were leaving Douala. As a result, the border between the Republic of Congo and Zaire was closed, and the Air France airliner was forced to land in Brazzaville. There it appeared that, although we had tickets, we were not on the passenger list. So we were left alone in the airport as the other passengers were taken off to a hotel in the city. The lights went out and the mosquitoes arrived in droves.

The following morning, with the aid of a Belgian fellow passenger who was desperate to get to Kinshasa and an East German crop-dusting pilot based in Brazzaville, we managed to board a pre-World War II plane and illegally cross to a deserted Kinshasa Airport. Once we'd made it into the city I was able to contact Mort Rosenblum of Associated Press, for whom I'd done some work, and we had a few days respite thanks to him and his wife, Sue.

We were concerned about our lack of funds, so, having paid a bribe for a backdated entry visa, we decided not to wait for connecting flights and instead flew from Kinshasa to Lubumbashi, near the Zambian border. From there we thought we could hitch-hike the rest of the way. It wasn't that easy. After being robbed at gunpoint by a drunken Zairean soldier and stranded on the border for half a day, we eventually made it to Ndola, courtesy of a Czech geologist and a Zambian taxi driver.

At last we were back in southern Africa, where we wished to be. Before long I landed a job as features editor at the *Times of Zambia* and in December our parents were able to drive to Ndola to spend Christmas with us. Despite my initial trepidation, we all got on surprisingly well, especially considering our political differences. The following year our daughter, Ceiren, was born and we planned to settle in Zambia until we could finally return to South Africa.

That should have been the end of the story. But once again political machinations beyond our control got us on the move.

Following the detente talks between President Kenneth Kaunda of Zambia and South Africa's apartheid Prime Minister, John Vorster, work permits for ANC members working in Zambia were not renewed. I was not welcome in Botswana either. However, there were jobs available in New Zealand. ANC acting president Oliver Tambo and his close confidant, Jack Simons, felt that if we could not stay in Botswana we should go to New Zealand to help support and build an anti-apartheid movement.

So it was that, in 1971, Barbara, our daughter and I settled in New Zealand or, as the Maori people called it, Aotearoa — Land of the Long White Cloud. Our son, Brendan, was born there in 1972, the year that activists in that country launched what became, per capita, the largest anti-apartheid movement in the world. I was proud to be invited to be the keynote speaker at that launch.

It was a fascinating, sometimes turbulent and very productive period in our lives. With our two children, a dog and a cat, we spent sixteen months living on the road in a 10-metre (36-foot) bus. We campaigned on various issues and I wrote the *whakapapa* (genealogy) of the Ngati Whatua Maori people. While starting and operating a major news feature agency, I also wrote two books, several booklets and chapters on social studies and history for schools. With Barbara, I helped to run and teach at an experimental primary school, and was part of the nine-year campaign that finally gained a free pardon and $1 million compensation for Arthur Allan Thomas, who had been wrongly convicted of a double murder. In between I met, interviewed and wrote about characters as diverse as Peter Cook and Dudley Moore, Arnold Palmer and Theodor Seuss Geisel (Dr Seuss).

And in all the time since giving up our canoeing venture in Arenys de Mar, there was only one occasion when — alone this time — I ventured into a kayak again: during a "peace squadron" blockade of the US nuclear submarine *Haddo* in Auckland harbour in 1979. That vessel turned out to have a bigger bow wave than anything Barbara and I had encountered on the Rhône. But those protests, during which I ended up being arrested, resulted in New Zealand becoming the world's first nuclear-free zone.

By this time, feeling that we'd done all we could in New Zealand and wanting to be back in Africa, we wrote to Oliver Tambo asking if there was some contribution we could make closer to home. He replied immediately and asked us to come to Tanzania to start a primary school at the Solomon Mahlangu Freedom College (Somafco), set up to cater for the most recent flood of exiles following the political upheavals in South Africa in June 1976.

So it was that in August 1980 — thirteen years, two children and two continents later than planned — we finally arrived in Dar es Salaam, en route to Morogoro and the school at Mazimbu.

"Better late than never," said Barbara.

Culinary canoeing

by Barbara Bell

Most people, when hearing about our crazy canoe trip, tend to ask what and how we ate while travelling. When we finally agreed that the trip was on, Terry and I came to an arrangement: I would handle the catering; he would take care of the overall preparation for the kayak and the voyage. I had developed an interest in food while studying dietetics in South Africa and, shortly after arriving in London, an Indian friend introduced me to the use of herbs and spices in Asian cooking. This had an obvious influence on what I took with me in the kayak.

I soon realised that my greatest problems would be space and budget. To keep our strength up, we would need nutritious food that was both fresh and easy to prepare. This required careful planning if we were to survive the trip without too much stress — or even malnutrition. And mostly we would cook in one pot. It was going to be quite a challenge.

This was to be a long journey and I was restricted by lack of space and limited utensils. Also, this was fifty years ago and the equipment available was not as sophisticated as it is today. I have included here an idea of what we took with us and have provided some recipes I used. A few are my own, some are adapted from memory and others were given to me as we travelled. Recipes don't change, so our experiences may be useful to the adventurous hiker, canoeist or anyone travelling by caravan or houseboat or, indeed, on foot.

Eating was always enjoyable on those travels half a century ago — largely, I think, because of where we were. It was easy to eat with enthusiasm when local cheeses, breads, olives and pâtés were always of quality — and delicious. As was the variety of fruit and vegetables. For the first time in our experience, we bought ropes of onions and garlic, along with bunches of fresh herbs.

Especially in France, we often found ourselves close to markets where the helpful stallholders seemed to have no problem with the shoppers — mostly women — who prodded, squeezed, examined and smelled everything on offer before purchasing. It was a refreshing experience after the generally grumpy behaviour we encountered at London markets.

The variety of foods was wonderful and, to us in those days, quite exotic. I remember the barrels of anchovies, gherkins and wide array of cheeses from every region. In South Africa in my youth, the only cheese I recall my mother buying was what was known as sweet milk (a sort of Gouda) and third-grade Cheddar, a strong cheese that seemed to be used mostly for cooking. I only discovered recently that this was because the South African Dairy Board, until the 1980s, regulated prices and gave no scope for innovation.

In France I also discovered goats' cheese for the first time. It remains one of my favourites to this day. Then there were the meats and fish and, of course, sausages and salami — saucisson and chorizo — that became a significant part of our diet.

We noticed that the price of eating at restaurants and cafés was generally way above our budget, so our meals were a do-it-yourself affair and I was committed to regular cooking.

A canoe kitchen

Our equipment and supplies included:

- A paraffin stove bought in London, supplemented by a single-ring gas camping stove in France.
- Three different-sized billy cans with lids, all fitting into each other. The larger two were for cooking and the smaller one useful for boiling water. The lids doubled as frying pans or even containers for salads, nuts and olive, etc.

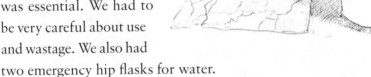

- Two water bottles of 2.5 litres each. Potable water was essential. We had to be very careful about use and wastage. We also had two emergency hip flasks for water.
- One medium-sized plastic bowl for salads or mixing. A colander slightly smaller than the bowl fitted into it and held small cans and bottles.
- One large plastic container used for washing up or turned upside down for use as a work surface. In it we stored supplies such as tinned baked beans, tinned corned beef, tinned sardines and mackerel, lentils, dried fruit and a small jar of mustard. At an army surplus store in London we bought a tin of "hard tack" emergency rations (never eaten) that probably dated from World War II.
- A smaller plastic box with powdered milk, tea bags and instant coffee, a few packets of soup, some rice and pasta, a little olive oil, a little vinegar, and a small jar of honey. This fitted into the large plastic container.
- A small glass jar with a lid, in which to mix salad dressing.
- Plastic film canisters that contained herbs and spices. Mainly in

France, fresh herbs were available, but we carried some dried basil, thyme, marjoram and oregano. Among the spices were garam masala, turmeric, paprika, cinnamon, cardamom, coriander and cloves. Of course, we also took salt and black pepper.

- Three enamel mugs; 4 enamel plates; 2 teaspoons, 2 dessert spoons, 2 forks, 2 knives and 1 tablespoon; a bread knife, a cook's knife and a paring knife; one small potato masher (very useful when making soup); a small measuring jug; a light plastic cutting board; two wooden spoons; a small strainer; a can opener; and a corkscrew.
- One small bottle of dishwashing liquid, a pot scourer and a few dish towels. On river and canal banks and on the seashore we usually scoured our pots with sand and never threw dirty water into the waterway.
- A torch and extra batteries, a packet of candles, a few boxes of matches wrapped in plastic, toilet paper and a little trowel.

Canoe fare

Breakfasts

If we were near villages or towns in France, we often bought a fresh baguette, croissants or brioches and enjoyed them with milky coffee, followed by anything left over from the night before, warmed up. Anything seemed to taste good, sitting on the water's edge on a fresh, early morning. In Spain it was usually fruit, bread and cheese or fried-dough pastries rolled in sugar called churros.

Lunches

Especially at sea, when we ate on the water, lunch was usually a snack — perhaps some olives, nuts, and dried or fresh fruit. In fact, fresh fruit was almost always a feature. Ashore, while travelling down the canals, we would eat whatever was available, and there was a great variety: cheese, tapenade, pâté, olives, gherkins and bread.

Evening meals

I tried to make these meals as nutritious as possible, buying food as we needed it. However, we always had some vegetables aboard such as onions, carrots and cauliflower, all of which carry well. Along with these we often had salami, packets of soup, spices and some rice or pasta. With these bare essentials a decent meal can always be prepared reasonably quickly.

Some tips

When cooking rice I always used one of our enamel mugs to measure quantities. The mug measured 250 g (1 cup). I used the absorption method of one mug of rice to 2 mugs of water, which works well. Using the 1 mug = 1 cup measurement, I often spiced up the rice by using a stock cube (any flavour) in the cooking water. With plain rice we always enjoyed eating leftovers with sugar and milk for breakfast.

When cooking bacon I always lined the pan with tinfoil. This made cleaning easy. It is worth remembering that bacon lasts a few days out of a fridge and travels well.

Cheese also keeps well if wrapped in a cloth that has been soaked in vinegar and then dried.

Packet soups are a boon. A tablespoon of packet soup can thicken and flavour any soup or stew. They are also a great standby, but cooking with fresh vegetables, meat or fish is definitely preferable.

In France and Spain fresh herbs were usually sold in bunches or half bunches, so in the recipes that follow I have often mentioned a bunch or a half bunch, but the amount of herbs used is a matter of personal taste.

While travelling, although it was just the two of us, I usually cooked for four. Leftovers were often eaten for breakfast or held until lunch.

A SELECTION OF RECIPES

FRANCE

Well 'allo," said the onion, "I've just come from France."
The asparagus swooned, she was all in a trance.
The beetroot turned red, she was quite in a flap,
For this Gallic onion was a most handsome chap.

Conflans tomato and pepper stew

Two weeks out from London, at Conflans, when I was still adjusting to the unusual cooking conditions, I made this simple vegetable stew, served with crusty French bread. It went down a treat.

2 tablespoons olive oil	4 peeled and chopped tomatoes
1 large finely chopped red onion	(or 400 g tin of same)
2 cloves crushed/chopped garlic	2 tablespoons sherry/red wine
2 chopped red peppers	2 teaspoons brown sugar
1 large chopped green pepper	1 tablespoon packet soup in a little water
1 teaspoon paprika	as stock (I used brown onion)
1 teaspoon mixed herbs	salt and pepper to taste
½ mug/cup pitted black olives	2 tablespoons yoghurt

METHOD:

Heat the oil and add the onion. Cook over low heat until the onion is soft. Add the garlic. Then add the peppers and cook over low heat for 15 minutes, stirring continuously. Remove from heat, add the paprika and herbs and stir in the tomatoes, sherry/wine, brown sugar and olives. Add the stock and seasoning. Cover and cook at reduced heat for about 20/25 minutes or until the vegetables are tender. Add yoghurt and serve with crusty bread for dipping.

Island camping bolognaise

This is what we ate after our first shopping expedition in Paris, where we could boast — as perhaps few people can — that we stayed on our own island in that city.

few slices bacon (if available)
1 chopped onion
2 cloves chopped garlic
2 chopped carrots
500 g minced meat
½ mug/cup dry white wine
400 g tin peeled, chopped tomatoes or

4 large peeled and chopped fresh
　tomatoes
2 teaspoons tomato purée
375 ml beef stock
1 teaspoon mixed herbs or small bunch
　fresh herbs
salt and pepper to taste

METHOD:

Fry the bacon with the chopped onion, garlic and carrots. Add the minced meat and wine and cook until the meat browns. Add the tomatoes, purée and stock. Add the herbs and salt and pepper, and simmer for at least an hour. Serve with pasta of your choice.

Consolation Island mushroom crêpes

This was the second meal on "our island", after the visit to the famous Les Halles market and after we discovered the theft of our tent. We bought six freshly cooked crêpes at the market and this is the recipe for the mushroom filling.

2 tablespoons olive oil
1 finely chopped onion
1 finely chopped garlic clove
1 tablespoon finely chopped marjoram
　or oregano or heaped teaspoon dried
　mixed herbs
goodly (about 5/6 tablespoons) glug of
　red wine

500 g thinly sliced button mushrooms
2 tablespoons plain flour
½ mug/cup chicken stock
grated cheese for sprinkling
salt and pepper to taste

METHOD:

Heat the oil, then the add onion and garlic, and cook gently until pale gold. Add the herbs and then pour in the red wine. Cook until the wine evaporates. Add the mushrooms and cook until they start to ooze juice. Continue to cook until all but about 2 tablespoons of juice have evaporated. Sprinkle the flour over, stir and then add the chicken stock. Bring to the boil, stirring, then cook for about 10 minutes until thick and creamy. Heat the crêpes, fill with the mixture and sprinkle with cheese.

Chicken anniversaire

1 tablespoon olive oil
4 peeled and chopped shallots
2 cloves chopped garlic
3 peeled and chopped carrots
2 bay leaves
1 teaspoon dried thyme (a few sprigs fresh thyme)
2 teaspoons lemon juice
6 skinless chicken pieces

1 mug/cup dry white wine
400 g tin chopped and peeled tomatoes or 4 large chopped and peeled fresh tomatoes
250 g chopped mushrooms
1 mug/cup chicken stock
handful of pitted black olives
small bunch chopped parsley
salt and pepper to taste

METHOD:

Heat the olive oil and sauté the shallots, garlic and carrots. Add the bay leaves, thyme, lemon juice and chicken pieces. Brown well. Pour in the wine and add the tomatoes, mushrooms and chicken stock. Allow to simmer, covered, for about 30 minutes or until the chicken is coloured and tender. Stir in the olives and chopped parsley. Season to taste. The meal should then be ready to serve with cooked rice (preferably without any pollutants).

Vegetarian Digoin

Stuck in Digoin after a pricey visit to the doctor to sort out Terry's torn muscle, we worried about our budget. As a result, we ate a lot of vegetables and, of course, fruit. We were there for some time and these are some of the vegetarian recipes I used.

Spicy vegetable pilau

175 g peas (fresh or frozen)
2 tablespoons olive oil
1 teaspoon garam masala
1 teaspoon turmeric
½ teaspoon cayenne pepper
175 g scrubbed and diced carrots
175 g cleaned and thinly sliced leeks
1 clove crushed/chopped garlic

175 g rice
275 g vegetarian stock (for non-vegetarian dish chicken stock may be used)
pinch chilli powder (optional)
50 g raisins
salt and pepper to taste
25 g desiccated coconut (optional)

METHOD:

Cook fresh or frozen peas and put aside. Heat the oil, add the spices and fry for a couple of minutes. Add the leeks, carrots, garlic and rice, and fry for a further 5 minutes. Add the stock and bring to the boil. Cook over gentle heat for 25 to 30 minutes until the rice is tender. Stir in the raisins, season to taste, add chilli if desired, and add the cooked peas. Sprinkle with desiccated coconut if using and serve. Heat oil, add the spices and fry for a couple of minutes.

Warm leek salad

About 675 g trimmed and chopped leeks
4 tablespoons olive oil
1 tablespoon vinegar
2 teaspoons Dijon mustard
½ teaspoon sugar

salt and pepper to taste
2 hard-boiled and chopped eggs
100 g black olives
1 tablespoon chopped parsley

METHOD:

Cook the leeks in salted boiling water for about 10 minutes until tender. Drain well. Return the leeks to pot and let them dry off in the heat. Make the dressing by mixing the oil and vinegar, then stirring in the mustard and sugar until smooth. Season well. Arrange the leeks in a dish and pour over the dressing. Sprinkle the eggs, olives and parsley over the leeks and serve.

Chickpea salad

Chickpeas are extremely nutritious. They contain plenty of good carbohydrates as well as protein, phosphorus, calcium and iron, and are said to have been the marching rations for the Arab armies as they moved into North Africa and Spain.

500 g tinned chickpeas
salt and pepper to taste
4 tablespoons olive oil
juice of one lemon
2 finely chopped spring onions

handful of rocket or parsley leaves,
    roughly chopped
100 g stoned black olives
100 g diced feta cheese

METHOD:

Place the chickpeas in a dish and season lightly with salt and pepper. Stir in the oil and lemon juice. Add the remaining ingredients. Stir gently into the mixture. Put aside for at least half an hour for the flavours to develop.

Puy (or brown) lentil salad

It's a good idea to prepare the dressing beforehand.

Dressing
100 ml olive oil
3 tablespoons vinegar (preferably red wine)
2 teaspoons Dijon mustard
2 small cloves crushed garlic
seasoning to taste
if available, 2 teaspoons soy sauce

Salad ingredients
250 g Puy or brown lentils
1 chopped red onion
1 red pepper, deseeded and diced
½ bunch finely chopped parsley
salt and pepper to taste

METHOD:

Mix together all the dressing ingredients and set aside. Place the lentils in a pan, cover with water and bring to the boil. Boil for 5 minutes, then reduce heat and simmer for 20 minutes until tender. Drain the lentils thoroughly and return to the pan. Stir in the dressing and leave to cool, stirring occasionally so the lentils absorb the dressing evenly. When cold, stir in the red onion, pepper and parsley. Season to taste and serve.

Saint-Gilles savoury scramble

I might have cooked this just outside Saint-Gilles had I not had too much rosé wine to drink.

1 tablespoon olive oil
1 large chopped onion
4 rashers chopped bacon
3 small sliced courgettes

1 small chopped red pepper
2 large peeled and chopped ripe tomatoes
4 eggs
salt and pepper to taste

METHOD:

Heat the oil, add the onion and bacon, and fry until both are cooked. Add the courgettes and pepper and cook for about 3 minutes. Add the tomatoes and cook for another 5 minutes. Mix the eggs, salt and pepper in a bowl. Add to the courgette mixture and cook, scrambling with a fork. Serve immediately with fresh bread (or toast, if available).

Narbonne Plage curry

This was our pre-Mistral meal.

2 tablespoons oil
1 chopped onion
1 teaspoon each of coriander, turmeric
and masala
1 teaspoon chopped root ginger
1 clove of crushed garlic
2 sliced carrots
3 sliced courgettes

1 small cauliflower
150 ml vegetable stock (chicken
or beef can be used)
100 ml yoghurt
handful of chopped cashew nuts
(if available)
salt and pepper to taste

METHOD:

Heat the oil, add the onion and fry until soft. Add the spices and garlic, and cook for a further few minutes. Add the carrots and courgettes, and fry for 2 to 3 minutes while stirring. Add salt and pepper to taste, along with the stock. Cover and simmer for 10 minutes. Break the cauliflower into florets, add and cook for a further 10 minutes. Stir in the nuts and yoghurt and heat through gently. Serve with rice or with bread for dunking.

Hot potato salad

This is a convenient accompaniment to any meal. We occasionally ate this salad with pan-fried fish bought fresh.

600 g potatoes (no need to peel)
2 sliced spring onions
1 ½ tablespoons chopped parsley
salt and pepper to taste

4 tablespoons olive oil
1 teaspoon Dijon mustard
1 tablespoon vinegar of your choice

METHOD:

Boil the potatoes until soft. Drain and cool slightly before placing in a bowl with spring onions, parsley and seasoning to taste. Make the dressing by combining oil, mustard and vinegar in a mug. Pour over and serve.

Camping vin chaud (Glühwein)

After a day of paddling and an early meal, a few glasses of *vin chaud*, or mulled wine, can be a real treat. It can get cold camping on the water's edge.

750 ml red wine
1 ½ tablespoons sugar or honey
3-4 whole cloves

1 stick cinnamon
3-4 slices of lemon or
   orange

METHOD:
Heat the wine, but do not boil as the alcohol will evaporate. Stir in sugar or honey. Add lemon/orange slices, cinnamon and cloves. Keep heated, but not boiling, for about 30 minutes. Strain and enjoy.

Aigues-Mortes cuisine

During our time in Aigues-Mortes I was given several recipes. In our makeshift kitchen in the asparagus fields, I was able to stand up to cook. This meant that I could handle recipes that were slightly more complicated. Unfortunately, asparagus was not in season at the time.

Tomato pilaf with bacon and avocado
(vegetarians: omit the bacon)

1 tablespoon olive oil
100 g finely chopped bacon
3 finely chopped shallots
1 clove crushed/finely chopped garlic
250 g long-grained rice (1 mug/cup)
2 skinned, deseeded and chopped
   tomatoes

500 ml (2 mugs/cups) vegetable stock
salt and pepper to taste
1 avocado, peeled, stoned and cut into
   cubes

METHOD:

In a saucepan, fry bacon in a little oil until lightly golden and crispy. Lift out and set aside. Soften the shallots and garlic in the same pan, without allowing them to brown. Stir in the rice and fry briskly for a few minutes, stirring continuously. Add the tomato flesh and stir over a moderate heat for a few minutes until the tomatoes have dried out a little. Pour in the stock and add salt and pepper to taste. Cover and cook for 15 to 16 minutes. Lift the lid and taste the rice. The stock should all be absorbed and the rice should be *al dente*. Just before serving, fork in the avocado cubes and the reserved bacon.

Sunset lamb cutlets Provençale

4 tablespoons breadcrumbs
1 teaspoon salt
½ teaspoon pepper
8 trimmed lamb cutlets
1 beaten egg
oil for shallow frying
2 tablespoons chopped parsley

Provençale sauce
2 tablespoons olive oil
1 sliced onion
1 red and 1 green sliced and seeded pepper
4 skinned tomatoes
1 clove finely chopped garlic
1 teaspoon tomato purée
1 teaspoon chopped thyme
salt and pepper to taste

METHOD:

Mix breadcrumbs with salt and pepper. Brush the cutlets with the beaten egg and roll in the breadcrumbs, pressing on well. Put aside.

For the sauce, heat the oil. Add the onion and peppers and fry until softened. Cut the tomatoes into eighths and add to the onion and peppers. Add the remaining ingredients, with salt and pepper to taste. Cover and simmer for 10 minutes or until the vegetables are soft.

For the cutlets, pour the oil into a pan and place over moderate heat. When the oil is hot, add the cutlets and fry for 4 to 5 minutes on each side until tender and golden brown. Drain off excess oil. Arrange cutlets on a plate, spoon over the sauce and sprinkle with chopped parsley. Serve with rice, pasta or couscous.

Carrots with salami and raisins

1 tablespoon oil
10 thin slices spicy salami, cut into strips
6 medium carrots, finely chopped
4 sliced spring onions

½ teaspoon cumin
½ teaspoon ground cinnamon
½ mug/cup raisins
¼ cup pine nuts

METHOD:

Heat the oil and add the salami, carrots, spring onions, cumin and cinnamon. Cook over low heat until the carrots are tender. Add the raisins and cook for 3 minutes longer. Then add the pine nuts and shake the pot to combine.

French bean salad

This salad is best dressed with a simple olive oil, lemon juice, salt and pepper dressing that was given to me by a stallholder in Aigues-Mortes. Use 3 big spoons of olive oil for every 1 to 2 big spoons of lemon juice, with salt and pepper to taste. A standard dressing (below) can be used.

50 g green beans
250 g mushrooms
3 avocados

small bunch parsley
Dressing

METHOD:

Top and tail the beans and cook in salted boiling water for 5 to 8 minutes. Drain and leave to cool. Wash and dry the mushrooms and cut them into fine slices. Peel the avocados, cut them in half and remove the pips, then cut them into tiny slices. Place the beans, mushrooms and avocado in a bowl. Add dressing and sprinkle with fresh parsley. Don't turn the salad until serving.

Standard salad dressing
4 tablespoons olive oil
1 tablespoon red wine vinegar/lemon
   juice or vinegar of your choice

1 teaspoon mustard
1 teaspoon honey
salt and black pepper to taste

A FLAVOUR OF SPAIN

Spain is a fascinating mix of people,
languages, culture and food, but if there is one thing
all Spaniards share, it's a love of food and drink.

So said the Spanish-American chef José Andrés. And there is nothing to beat a good chorizo, although, like other national sausages, there are many regional varieties. Chorizo travels well, too, and many of our kayaking meals were based on it, or on the spicy French saucisson. Spanish chorizo is generally made with smoked pork seasoned with smoked paprika, often with garlic and herbs. Thick cured saucisson, which we discovered in France, is usually made with lean pork, pork fat, spices, salt and sugar, although again, there are a great many regional varieties.

Cheat canoe cassoulet

This was our consolation meal when we returned from Portbou, after our experience with lice, to discover that our tent and stove had been stolen.

2 tablespoons olive oil
1 chopped onion
2 finely chopped garlic cloves
400 g tinned chopped tomatoes or 4
    large skinned and chopped fresh
    tomatoes
1 teaspoon mixed herbs or half bunch

fresh herbs
1 sliced chorizo or spicy Toulouse sausage
200 ml chicken or vegetable stock
2 finely chopped red chillies (optional)
salt and pepper to taste
2 tins (800 g) rinsed and drained butter
    or haricot beans

METHOD:

Heat oil in a pot and sauté the onion and garlic until soft. Add all the remaining ingredients (except the beans) and bring to the boil. Reduce heat and simmer for 20 minutes, adding the beans towards the end. Serve with crusty French/Spanish bread.

(For a vegetarian version replace the sausage with mushrooms, aubergines, red peppers or courgettes).

Chorizo stew

400 g chorizo sausage
200 ml red wine
400 g peeled and chopped tomatoes
400 g chickpeas (garbanzo)
2 cloves chopped garlic

few sprigs rosemary
2 teaspoons lemon juice and pinch of
    sugar
½ bunch parsley
salt and pepper to taste

METHOD:
Fry the sausage for 4 to 5 minutes. Pour in the wine. Add the rosemary and garlic, tomatoes and chickpeas. Simmer for 15 to 20 minutes. Add lemon juice, salt and pepper to taste and a pinch of sugar. Stir in parsley. Serve with Spanish crusty bread.

Garbanzos (chickpea) and chicken stew

2 tablespoons olive oil
6 chicken pieces (preferably thighs)
1 chopped onion and two cloves
    chopped garlic
1 diced red onion
1 diced red pepper

400 g tin skinned and chopped tomatoes
½ mug/cup dry white wine
½ mug/cup chicken stock
1 teaspoon masala
400 g tin chickpeas

METHOD:
Heat the oil and cook the chicken until golden brown, turning once. Remove from the pot. Add the onion, garlic and red pepper, and cook until the onion is soft. Add the tomatoes, wine, chicken stock and masala. Simmer for about 10 minutes. Add the chicken and chickpeas (drained) and cook until the chicken is tender and the vegetables are soft. Enjoy with rice, pasta or couscous.

Chorizo and rice soup

2 tablespoons olive oil
1 onion
1 clove chopped garlic
150 g sliced chorizo
1 mug/cup rice

1 mug/cup red wine
1.5 litres water and 1 cube chicken stock
400 g tin peeled and chopped tomatoes
    or 4 large peeled and chopped fresh
    tomatoes

METHOD:

Sauté the onions, garlic and chorizo for about 8 minutes. Add the rice and stir for about 2 minutes. Add the wine and 1 mug/cup of stock. Stir for a few minutes. Add the rest of the stock and tomatoes and cook for about 20 minutes.

Savoury rice

This can be served with any meat or fish dish instead of plain boiled rice.

1 ½ tablespoons olive oil
1 chopped onion
1 mug/cup uncooked rice
2 mugs/cups water

2 peeled and chopped tomatoes
½ teaspoon sugar
salt and pepper to taste

METHOD:

Heat the oil and fry the onion until soft, but not brown. Add rice and fry for about 2 minutes, stirring constantly. Add the tomato, sugar, salt and pepper, and water. Bring to the boil. Reduce heat, cover and simmer for about 20 minutes or until the rice is cooked and all the liquid has been absorbed.

Tomato and chorizo salad

6 medium-sized fresh tomatoes
4 finely chopped spring onions
pinch of sugar
½ bunch chopped parsley
8 slices chorizo/salami

2 cloves finely chopped garlic
3 tablespoons olive oil
1 ½ tablespoons vinegar (preferably red
    wine)
salt to taste

METHOD:

Chop the tomatoes into quarters and thinly slice the onions. Place in a bowl with parsley and the pinch of sugar. In a pot, fry the salami in a little oil, then add the sliced garlic and fry lightly. Add the vinegar and the rest of the olive oil. Finally, add to tomatoes in bowl and allow to cool. Season and serve.

MOROCCAN MUSINGS

Although it is just one hour away by boat from Spain, Morocco is a world away from Europe. The years of Spanish and French colonisation could not entirely displace an ancient culture.

Troth Wells

I found Moroccan cuisine fascinating, especially since much of the cooking in that country is done in one pot, just what I had to deal with during our journeying. I obviously had to include the one-pot meal provided for us by the travelling desert salesman. I tried to memorise and copy that meal and what I list here is at least a close approximation.

In those days before pre-cooked couscous, he would have used a coarsely ground wheat, rolled in flour and already cooked by steaming, that he probably bought in the market. I found it too difficult to cope with this while travelling, but today pre-cooked couscous is readily available and is a good substitute for rice or pasta in most dishes.

Salesman's spicy lamb stew

500 g stewing lamb
1 finely chopped onion
1 clove finely chopped garlic
1 kg tomatoes, peeled and cut into pieces
salt and pepper to taste
½ teaspoon saffron powder or turmeric
¼ teaspoon ginger

1 teaspoon cinnamon
1 teaspoon cumin
4 peeled and diced turnips
3 peeled and diced sweet potatoes
juice of one lemon
handful of olives and bunch of finely
   chopped coriander

METHOD:

Put the meat into the pot or billy can with the onion, garlic and tomatoes, and cover with water. Bring to the boil and remove any scum. Add the salt and pepper and spices and cook, covered, for about an hour until the meat is very tender. Then add the rest of the ingredients and cook for 15 to 20 minutes or until the vegetables are tender. Serve on rice or couscous.

Harissa

I was intrigued by harissa, the fiery paste used in many North African dishes. This paste can also be enjoyed — in small quantities — in most stews and soups and can even be eaten on toast, although not by the faint-hearted. I did not cook it on the trip as I had no oven, but thought I should include a recipe.

3 red peppers
4 red chillies (the hotter the better)
4 cloves crushed garlic
4 teaspoons tomato purée
2 teaspoons olive oil

juice of one lemon
1 teaspoon cumin
2 teaspoons coriander
½ teaspoon ground cinnamon
salt and pepper to taste

METHOD:

Put the peppers on a tray and roast them near top of the oven at 200°C until soft and blistered (about 30 minutes). After 15 minutes add the chillies. When cooked, cover with foil and once cooled, remove the pepper skins and cut them up. Put the peppers, chillies, garlic, tomato purée, salt and pepper, lemon juice and spices in a blender and blitz until smooth. Season with salt, pepper and olive oil. Keep in the fridge for a few weeks. Eat with couscous dishes, curries, stews, pizzas, grilled meat, fish dishes and roasted vegetables.

Minted pea soup

1 tablespoon olive oil
4/5 finely chopped spring onions
1 crushed/chopped garlic clove
500 g fresh/frozen peas

½ bunch finely chopped fresh mint
1 litre vegetable or chicken stock
25 ml fresh cream
salt and pepper to taste

METHOD:

Heat the oil and fry the onions and garlic until softened. Add the peas and mint and stir fry for about 10 minutes. Add the stock and bring to the boil. Remove from heat and mash until smooth. Stir in the cream and season to taste. Return to heat and heat through. Serve topped with a dollop of cream and a sprinkle of chopped mint.

North African lentil soup

2 tablespoons olive oil
2 chopped onions
6 chopped carrots
2 chopped/crushed garlic cloves
1 teaspoon cumin
1 teaspoon coriander

2 tablespoons tomato paste
250 ml/1 mug red wine
1 ¼ mugs chicken or vegetable stock
250 ml/1 mug brown (or Puy) lentils
small bunch chopped fresh mint
salt and pepper to taste

METHOD:

Heat the oil and sauté the carrots and onions over low heat for about 10 minutes. Stir in the garlic, spices and tomato paste and cook for a few minutes. Add the wine and boil for a further 2 to 3 minutes. Add the stock and lentils. Simmer, partially covered, for 60 minutes. Add seasoning, stir in the mint and serve.

Spicy parsnip/carrot soup

2 tablespoons olive oil
1 chopped onion
1 chopped/crushed garlic clove
½ teaspoon turmeric
¼ teaspoon chilli powder

450 g chopped parsnips/carrots or
    a mixture of both
1.2 litres (5 mugs) vegetable stock
salt and pepper to taste

METHOD:

Heat the oil and cook the onion until soft. Add the garlic, turmeric and chilli powder. Cook for a few minutes. Add the parsnips/carrots and stir well. Pour in the stock and bring to the boil. Cover and simmer for about 20 minutes. Cool the soup and purée with masher (or liquidiser if available). Heat again and season with salt and pepper.

Potatoes with cumin

This is a Moroccan way to cook potatoes. They can be served with any meat, fish or vegetarian dish.

2 tablespoons olive oil
1 diced red pepper
2 cloves crushed garlic
1 teaspoon ground cumin (little more if preferred)

1 kg potatoes, cut into chunks and parboiled
thinly sliced peel of half a lemon
2 tablespoons chopped parsley
salt and pepper to taste

METHOD:

Heat 1 tablespoon of oil and fry red pepper until softened. Add the garlic and cumin and stir. Add the potatoes and extra oil. Turn them around in the oil so that they brown on all sides. When they are almost ready, sprinkle in the lemon peel and season. Scatter parsley on top just before serving with yoghurt.

Camping mint tea

This recipe is in memory of the days in Morocco when we were first challenged to canoe from London to Dar es Salaam. It's worth buying some green China tea for this refreshing drink. Here is the recipe for tea for two:

2 mugs/cups water
2 teaspoons green China tea
honey/sugar to taste
¼ mug/cup chopped fresh mint sprigs

METHOD:

Pour water into a billy can and bring to the boil. Stir in the tea and honey or sugar to taste. Remove from heat, add the mint and let rest for about 10 minutes. Strain and enjoy.

Kayaking: know what you are doing

The Inuit — the "Eskimos" — paddled, travelled and hunted in kayaks for centuries. These highly manoeuvrable craft, with the centre of gravity below the waterline, made them extremely stable. Kayaks, in an adapted form, made their entry onto the world sporting stage in 1936, with kayak events at the Olympics in Berlin (although there had been "demonstration events" at the Olympics 12 years earlier). But it was only in the wake of World War II, and especially in the 1960s, that sport canoeing and kayaking, along with touring, began to move into the mainstream. In Britain, for example, national proficiency tests were only introduced at about that time. And proficiency is essential. We didn't have it, and only by dint of luck and labour did we become halfway competent.

Today, around the world, there are many canoe and kayak clubs and tests to achieve various levels of proficiency. To truly enjoy kayaking, whether for a day, a weekend or a longer tour, on a river, lake or along a coast, it is best to know exactly what you are doing and what to expect.

We had an interesting time, but it was often frightening in ways that it need not have been. We learned a lot, but much of this we could have — and should have — learned before we set out. Today, unfortunately, it is no longer possible to paddle a kayak through the waterways of France in the way we did. Perhaps the *"Bateau Amandla"* was the first in modern times — and the last.

Many of the waterways have also changed and the Rhône is no longer the heavily trafficked river it once was: it has been tamed by an extensive canal system. However, there are many other available waterways around the world that provide challenges at various levels, or even just a means to relax. Whatever the water — rapids, river, lake or sea — and whatever the kayak, it's best to be fully prepared in order to gain the maximum experience and enjoyment.

And it's always best to take a hat.

Recipe index

Cross references to Terry's text are given in **bold**.

Printed in the United States
By Bookmasters